Something Like A Drug

AN UNAUTHORIZED ORAL HISTORY OF THEATRESPORTS

Something Like A Drug

AN UNAUTHORIZED ORAL HISTORY OF THEATRESPORTS

KATHLEEN FOREMAN AND CLEM MARTINI

Red Deer College Press

THE PUBLISHERS
Red Deer College Press
56 Avenue & 32 Street Box 5005
Red Deer Alberta Canada T4N 5H5

ACKNOWLEDGEMENTS
Edited for the Press by Joyce Doolittle
Cover and text design by Dennis Johnson
Printed and bound in Canada for Red Deer College Press by Parkland ColourPress

The authors and editors thank Deborah Iozzi for her assistance with the photographs. Thanks also to John Bessemer for his assistance.

Financial support provided by the Alberta Foundation for the Arts, a beneficiary of the Lottery Fund of the Government of Alberta, and by the Canada Council, the Social Sciences and Humanities Research Council of Canada, the Department of Canadian Heritage, the University of Calgary Research Grants Committee and Red Deer College.

COMMITTED TO THE DEVELOPMENT OF CULTURE AND THE ARTS

DISCLAIMER
While all due care has been taken in the preparation of this book, the authors and editors cannot be held responsible for any errors or omissions contained herein, nor for any damage or injury arising from any interpretation of its contents, howeverso caused. Opinions expressed are those of the contributors and not necessarily those of the authors and editors.

CANADIAN CATALOGUING IN PUBLICATION DATA

Something like a drug
ISBN 0-88995-122-5

1. Improvisation (Acting)—History. I. Foreman, Kathleen Joyce,
1958- II. Martini, Clem, 1956-
PN2071.I5S65 1995 792'.028   C94-910899-5

LIBRARY OF CONGRESS CATALOGING-IN-PUBLICATION DATA

Something like a drug: an unauthorized oral history of theatresports / [edited] by Clem Martini and Kathleen Foreman.
p. cm.
ISBN 0-88734-918-8 (pbk. : alk. paper)
1. Improvisation (Acting) I. Foreman, Kathleen, 1958- II. Martini,
Clem.
PN2071.I5S58 1995 792'.028—DC20

To everyone who shared their stories with us, thank you.
–KF & CM

Foreword

Any chronicle of the history of theatresports must begin with the man responsible in so many ways for its development, Keith Johnstone. I was an associate professor in the Department of Drama at the University of Calgary when Keith was hired, the Loose Moose Theatre Company was formed and theatresports began. Keith's reputation as a brilliant acting teacher preceded him. Richard Courtney and Carl Hare, who had been his colleagues at the University of Victoria, recommended him highly. I even had a tiny role in inviting him to Calgary. When my involvement with the international association for theatre for children (ASSITEJ) took me to Venice and London in 1970, my boss, Victor Mitchell, asked me to see Johnstone's Theatre Machine and sound him out about a job in our department. I did and he was interested. Also, I was vaguely aware that Keith Johnstone had had something to do with Ann Jellicoe's play *The Knack,* which had been important in my own history. So I was really looking forward to having Keith as a colleague.

Keith joined the department as an instructor of acting in 1971. He left in 1972 but returned in 1975 as an assistant professor on the tenure track. During this period, I gradually became aware of a dedicated group of students working outside class hours with Keith and his wife, Ingrid, in free noontime improvisation and mask sessions—advertised on the department bulletin board as the Secret Impro Show. The core group performed, and audience members joined in if they were brave enough. I tried once.

Keith's group made marvelous masks. Some were faces cut

from magazines and mounted on cardboard. Some were papier–mâché. Some of the masked people of the Secret Improv Shows developed, over time, into unique characters reminiscent of the *commedia dell'arte*—the popular seventeenth century improvisational theatre that flourished in Italy, influenced Molière and bequeathed us such universal tricksters as Arlecchino (Harlequin) and Pulcinella (Punch). I particularly remember Dennis Cahill's wonderful masked character, Spaghetti, who combined vulnerability, guile and mayhem in a manner similar to the silent movie stars Buster Keaton and Charlie Chaplin.

Johnstone's games and strategies developed simultaneously with such popular phenomena as the *British Goon Show* and *Monty Python* in England and *Second City, Saturday Night Live* and *SCTV* in the USA and Canada. Small wonder then that Johnstone's iconoclastic style found fervent converts in those Calgary drama students who felt restricted by orthodox productions. They revelled in the controlled chaos of Johnstone's classes and workshops, and in the opportunity to create their own material.

Some of the games Keith taught his students reminded me of Viola Spolin's work and her book *Improvisation for the Theatre* (1963). She designed games to free actors from tensions blocking their creativity. Beginning in the Great Depression of the 1930s, Spolin worked for the U.S. government in "make work" projects for children and community theatres. She believed that drama was a good tool for self-expression and that one way to free people up, so they weren't "acting," was to give them a task or game.

Spolin's son, Paul Sills, was in his mother's classes and productions as a child. When he grew up, he went into the theatre, directing plays in Chicago. And then in the late fifties, using his and his mother's improvisation techniques, he founded a theatre, first called Compass and then The Second City. Alan Arkin, Mike Nichols and Elaine May were early alumni. From the Toronto off-shoot of Second City came the TV series *SCTV* and such successful film comics as Catherine O'Hare, John Candy, Andrea Martin and Dan Ackroyd.

But exciting new forms of improvisation weren't restricted to Chicago and Toronto. Keith's teaching in Calgary led to the establishment in 1977 of an improvisational theatre company—Loose Moose Theatre. It found a home at the Pumphouse Theatre, a low-rent performance space for emerging young professionals and innovative work.

In 1978 theatresports evolved from the activities of Loose Moose. To the amazement of everyone, it took very little time for word of this new theatre and sports hybrid to spread. Keith's many invitations to teach and direct in North America and abroad helped. His book *Impro: Improvisation and the Theatre* (1979) has become an important acting text and handbook for disciples eager to start their own companies. Some actors who started with Loose Moose in Calgary left town and began theatresports in other cities. Today, many alumni of theatresports and Loose Moose can be found around the world as performance artists, stand-up comedians, TV stars and playwrights, including two actor-writers of *Kids in the Hall*, Bruce McCullough and Mark McKinney.

In a way, theatresports is more populist and democratic than Second City. While actors from both Second City and theatresports talk about how valuable each has been in honing their skills as comedians, there are more entry points for ordinary people—more tolerance for amateurs—in theatresports.

Now Keith's work has intersected with mine again. Clem Martini and Kathleen Foreman were both his students and mine. Kathleen played Olga in my production of *Three Sisters,* and Clem played the fairy tale hero in the Russian children's play *The Dragon.* He also took my playwriting class. I've known them both for years. When they came to me with the idea to do an oral history of theatresports, I was intrigued. What better way to chronicle the life of this phenomenon than by conversation with people intimately involved with its origins and growing success. After all, conversation is everyone's improvisation.

–JOYCE DOOLITTLE
March 1995

Introduction

Clem Martini

It's the seventies and I'm studying drama. Who knows why. Everyone's studying drama in the seventies. Drama has become part of the youth movement. Street theatre, guerrilla theatre—you can't march to the corner store without a group doing performance art accompaniment. Anyway, anyway, for whatever reasons, I'm in drama, and I associate drama with intensity and life and urgency and contemporary existence, but . . . I am hard pressed in my first year at university to hold onto these illusions because nearly everything I see seems to indicate that theatre isn't urgent or alive and has nothing to do with contemporary life. I see the works of Shaw (dead) and Tennessee Williams (dead) and Shakespeare (quite dead), and everyone in these plays speaks in an accent different to mine, and all the concerns of these plays seem to be the concerns of people far, far away, and I wonder to myself, What have I been thinking?

Then I hear about Keith Johnstone.

He's teaching as a sessional instructor at the University of Calgary, and the students who take his classes find him fun, unintimidating and committed to a completely different kind of theatre. So as soon as I can—my second year—I register in his course.

Like most others in the course, I attend religiously because a missed class might mean . . . missing something important, something *vital*. I don't know what it is exactly, but magic is worked in that class. Every day is an emotional experience—

frustrating, energizing, enlightening. Each day something amazing happens. People creating drama out of thin air . . . out of *nothing*. My first encounter with improvisation.

And of course, along with the lessons, Keith has things to say. Things like, "Most of theatre performed today is deadly." Things like, "Why is it that there's no difficulty filling the seats at a sporting event, but the theatres are always crying for attendance?" This is the early seventies. Very little in the way of indigenous work is being done in Canada at this time. This is revolutionary talk.

So of course when I was invited to join Loose Moose Theatre and train at improvisational games late at night in an abandoned garage in a run-down portion of the city, I was thrilled. I remember thinking, This *is* a revolutionary act. I'd stolen *Steal This Book*. I'd heard, "If you're not part of the solution, you're part of the problem," and I believed it. I *believed* it! I thought what we were doing *was* part of the solution—for what ailed the theatre and maybe for what ailed society as a whole.

There's no doubt that the majority of the group felt . . . well . . . that we were conspiring at some sort of subversive operation. I think we were all mildly surprised that the police didn't take a more active interest in what we were doing.

As I write this, more than fifteen years have passed. I still improvise. It is, as others in the book will say, something like a drug—easy to get hooked on, hard to kick. Theatresports has become both less and more than what I'd expected. It's now played on a truly global scale on over three continents, and I find that . . . that size . . . that scale . . . an amazing development. It's amazing that so many improvisors whom I have known for so long still improvise so frequently and so well— often with little recognition for the quality of their work or their ability to maintain characters and a plot all spinning in the air like some sort of circus performer. It's amazing that theatresports has inveigled itself into the theatre world much like a virus—subtly and without introduction. And like a virus, it has popped up throughout the world in the most unlikely places.

But like any major enterprise or undertaking, theatresports has not turned out to be everything it was supposed to be.

Many of those involved in theatresports in the early days look askance at what the game has become. Even Keith Johnstone commented bitterly to me in my last interview with him, "I haven't made a penny off the game, and it's only in the last year or so that I've gotten any credit for it. Before that, the game was played so badly in so many places that it hurt my reputation more than it helped it."

For good or ill, it would appear that theatresports is here to stay. This book will try to explain in the words of those who were there how this odd exciting . . . thing . . . was created.

Kathleen Foreman

In the fall of 1977, the newly formed Loose Moose Theatre was doing what it called Free Impro shows at the Pumphouse Theatre. Keith Johnstone was beginning to experiment with the idea of theatresports, and my initiation into this theatrical experiment was partially based on pure logistics—he didn't have enough people in the company to fill all the emerging roles. With only six in the company, it was difficult to have two teams, judges and scorekeepers, and keep an eye on the whole process at the same time. The original team was already a tight improvisation group called the "Moose" team. I, along with three other new recruits, became the "Moosettes"—three slightly balding guys and a chick, and the first opposing theatresports team.

In the beginning I remember the laughter most of all. I had become involved with a group of people who got together and laughed like crazy. During the first year, we were spending probably twenty or so hours a week engaged in this spontaneous overdrive experiment. It was great! We had immersed ourselves in a spontaneity training that altered our brain waves, and we were high on it. We were "unblocking"—shedding habits, conventions, inhibitions and all sorts of educated reactions and cultural expectations as we investigated the transformational qualities of spontaneous improvisation.

While we learned to improvise we also discovered how to

make theatresports function. The private rehearsal period for this new theatre form was very short. I don't remember much about that first public theatresports game, but what I do recall is the incredible surge of energy and communication passing between the players and the audience. The audience acted the way they would at a sporting event! It was a totally outrageous thing to witness in a theatre. I had for the first time in my totally nonathletic existence found a sport I liked and could play.

Theatresports is now played around the world. The impact of spontaneous improvisation on my life is not an isolated story. The more you play, the more people you meet who talk about the work in similar ways. Everyone has a story to tell, and many begin with, "Someone told me to go see this 'thing,' this thing called *theatresports*. I'd never seen anything like it. I couldn't believe it, but I knew I wanted to try it."

Something Like a Drug is a collection of stories as told to us by members of the international community of theatresports players, ex-players and fans. Their memories capture an intriguing mixture of joy, terror and laughter, and they reflect the process that has supported the creation and evolution of theatresports.

Improvisation is a hard habit to break. I was present at the beginning of theatresports, and I am still an active improvisor. Theatresports is my team sport, but I improvise to keep my brain alive. I do it to keep connected to my art form. I do it with my impro family. I love it.

A Short Word On How This Book Is Organized

A few things should be cleared up at the outset of this oral history of theatresports. In the first place, what is theatresports? In the second place, what is an oral history?

To get to the first question first, it's not our place, not the place of this book, to describe theatresports in its entirety—to do so would require a whole other, different book, and in fact Keith Johnstone will be releasing just such a book soon. But for those who have never heard of or seen theatresports, it might be useful to give the game a quick going over.

As the name indicates, the game has attributes of both theatre and sport. Two teams of improvisors vie for control of the stage. A team gains stage time by performing the most entertaining scene and earning the most points from a panel of judges set up to adjudicate which team has performed more adeptly. In the end, the team with the most points—that is, the most entertaining team that evening—wins. (Theoretically, at least.)

Simple. Or perhaps not so simple. In fact, many variations of the game exist. There is the Danish Game—no judges and the audience decides who wins each set. There are Challenge Matches—one team alternately challenges the other team to a specific "game," and the judges rule on which team has won the challenge. Then the next team challenges and so on. There are also international permutations and spin-offs, and as more nations enter the league, it seems likely that even more variations on the basic format will emerge. Regardless of what rules are used, the fundamental premise is that entertainment wins out—the audience should be guaranteed a good night.

To answer the second question, an oral history involves examining any "thing" by using the actual words and observations of the people who saw or experienced this "thing." American historian Allan Nevins was one of the first historians to understand that contemporary society, accustomed as it is to global access to individuals via cars, airplanes and telephone lines, might no longer leave behind a testament of letters and journals as a basis for historical study. Since 1948 he, along with a number of associates from Columbia University, began to transcribe taped autobiographical accounts of prominent individuals. Another notable in this field has been Studs Terkel, who published several marvelous oral histories, including *Hard Times: An Oral History Of The Great Depression*, *The Good War: An Oral History of World War Two* and *Division Street, America*, an oral account of urban unrest. In a similar vein, *Something Wonderful Right Away* records the history of the Second City improvisational theatre group through interviews.

In our case, the "thing" in question is theatresports. The observers of this thing are all the theatresports participants we could contact and persuade to sit still and talk to us.

When we first thought about chronicling the history of theatresports, we knew it would have to be an oral history. The anecdotal form most closely paralleled the manner in which theatresports itself spread—through word of mouth, through stories passed on from one person to another.

In the process of recording our various interviews, we found that sometimes individuals held conflicting opinions about what had actually occurred over the years. When this happened, we opted to let the stories conflict and allow readers to discern the truth of the matter themselves. This seemed to us one of the strengths of the oral history form—it imposed fewer filters on participants' actual experience.

Once the interviews were transcribed, we edited solely to remove the inevitable redundancies and extraneous information that occur whenever one talks for an extended period. Following this, the transcripts were sent back to the interviewees for their approval.

In laying out this book, a natural order evolved. Keith Johnstone, the person most directly responsible for theatresports, seemed to require his own chapter. Keith received the two longest interviews, and ultimately he expressed the desire to extensively reedit them himself. They have become the first chapter and the opening section of the third chapter.

Stories from the original group of Calgary improvisors logically followed Keith's section. Some participants from that first group don't appear here—some have retired from theatresports and declined to be interviewed; some could no longer be found. But many of the first group do appear, and their stories describe the early years of the game.

The next logical section covers the first groups to create a truly national theatresports league.

Following closely on their heels are stories from international participants. These we reached while travelling to the United States, attending international theatresports competitions and visiting the international Impro Clinics held at Loose Moose. Considering the limited budget we had for travel and the far-flung nature of theatresports geography, we have managed to collect a fair representation of this international contingent.

In reviewing the manuscript as a whole, we discovered just how much jargon theatresports has accumulated over the years. A novice to the sport may experience some difficulty reading such a chronicle without a guide to relevant terms and concepts. For this reason, a glossary has been included at the back of the book.

We should also acknowledge that theatresports is a changing beast. There are always new players, and some who join one year are gone the next, so keeping up to date is difficult. In the time it has taken us to gather interviews for this book and see its publication, the theatresports scene will have already experienced small changes. Inevitably, as well, many theatresports people with interesting stories to tell never got the opportunity to share them. At least not with us. Our apologies to those we missed. Perhaps in another decade, theatresports will have changed so dramatically that a second oral history will be required.

Until then, hold that thought.

Genesis

THE PRESHOW CHAT

No single person can be credited more with theatresports' evolution than Keith Johnstone. He formed the first theatresports group, primarily with people at the University of Calgary where he taught, and he has helped establish theatresports groups around the world. Prior to coming to Calgary, Keith already had a long and illustrious (perhaps notorious) career in the theatre. He had worked at the London's Royal Court Theatre as a play reader, director and improvisation teacher. He had formed his own improvisational company called The Theatre Machine and had toured Europe. He had explored the improvisational form. When he came to Canada, he had certain notions and ideas in place about where, artistically, he would like to go next.

Keith Johnstone

Theatresports was inspired by the professional wrestling that I saw in the late fifties with William Gaskill and John Dexter. We thought of replacing wrestlers with improvisors, but every word and gesture on the stage had to be approved ahead of time by the Lord Chamberlain, a palace official. Because it's impossible to sue the Queen, there was nothing we could do, so theatresports was just a way to liven up my impro classes (it wasn't called theatresports then; it didn't have a name until I needed to advertise it). We'd play hat games or no-blocking games between teams, and sometimes we'd throw in a commentator, and in case of disputes we had three judges, but it didn't seem anything special at the time.

Wrestling was the only form of working-class theatre that existed. It clearly wasn't a sport because it was often presented on cinema stages and the expressions of agony were all played "out front." The content wasn't very interesting, but the audience was exactly the audience I wanted but didn't get in straight theatre. It was a family entertainment, and the audience was very loud—as important as the performers. Sometimes the wrestlers would clamp together like magnets and let the audience scream and howl for ten minutes.

When I tried theatresports in Canada, the class went wild with enthusiasm, whereas the English had treated it like Edwardian cricket. So one can say that Canadians were responsible for theatresports in that it was their enthusiasm that made it seem worthwhile. And in England I'd always worked with only a handful of improvisors, but in Canada I had twenty or more people desperate for stage time, and theatresports was a way of giving them stage time.

The very first version of theatresports did encourage bad feeling; and when teams have the same players month after month, their loyalty is to the team rather than to the Moose. I had invented a version of theatresports based on No Blocking—because I didn't believe that my "English" version was capable of sustaining an entire show (It is!). If the off-stage team yelled "block" (and the judges agreed), they replaced the on-stage team. But if the judges didn't agree, you lost ten points. The challenges were not scored— their purpose was to win time on stage in which to accumulate points. Winning a challenge gave you ten minutes of stage time. This was cruel because you could lose every challenge and could end up with minus two hundred points if you were overruled twenty times! And then the audience got to throw pies at you!

I introduced the pies to make a spectacular ending. Some supporters had been drifting off once it was clear that "their team" was going to lose, but after I introduced the pies, everyone stayed till the end. I wanted the pies to be made of shaving cream, but for month after month they used whipping cream that began to stink after twenty minutes (and there were no showers in the theatre). So they were suffering more than was necessary.

Another reason for the bad feeling in the early days is that players wanted to become famous instantly, and I kept saying that they'd have to leave Calgary for that to happen. And they wanted to be paid, but if we'd shared up the money the amount would have been derisory (we charged a dollar admission). Even now we pay only a few people—the business manager, director (not me), front of house, production manager. Canada Council still won't fund us, and it's now become clear to everyone that I was right when I said that to become famous you have to leave Calgary.

I remember people complaining angrily that my ideas were always accepted because of my "charisma," and that this wasn't fair! Yet I had to fight everyone when I introduced the Regular Game. People argued that if I scrapped the No Blocking rule then it wouldn't be theatresports anymore, but I'd played theatresports in England without the No Blocking rule, so I knew it would work. Yet I had to argue with person after person, including Mel Tonken [Keith's business partner]. No one wanted to alter what had worked so well when it was a novelty, even though I'd had to scrap it because the audience was no longer interested. It was either no theatresports or play the Regular Game.

The reason people believed that my ideas were usually accepted "automatically" is that, in general, I never fought for them. If I make a suggestion that doesn't inspire anyone, I make another suggestion. I don't believe in democracy in which people out-vote each other. If there isn't massive support for something, I'd rather produce another idea. I would produce idea after idea, and no one would even notice that they'd been rejected, whereas the average Canadian will get an idea and try to fight it through against massive opposition. I'm not sure my way is right, but I think it does account for the peculiar "looseness" of Loose Moose. There were only two ideas that I actually fought for—the introduction of the Regular Game and taking over the theatre. No, just one thing, because taking over the theatre was a *fait accompli.* We did it that way because Mel said he'd take the financial risk and because we'd already lost one theatre space because the "word got out." You could argue that if I were more bossy, Loose Moose would have achieved a lot more. But who knows. Most theatre companies would have collapsed long ago.

Theatresports is really just a lot of "Theatre Machines" [the improvisation group Keith founded in the sixties] all competing against each other. And most of the best games come from that time even though people now call them "classic" games as if they've always existed. I think the best improvisation games are usually mine. I'm very biased. I seldom like other people's games, although I adapt some of them, and of course anyone can challenge another team—even to the horrible "freeze" games that train improvisors to get laughs by killing stories.

The quickest way to improve standards would be to forbid groups to ask for a suggestion more than once every forty minutes. Accepting suggestions before every scene guarantees that most of the work will be rubbish. It's as if many groups have decided that storytelling is too difficult and have settled for being stupid instead. The spectators compete to see who can make the silliest suggestion, and a suggestion that gets a laugh is usually funnier than the scene it inspires. It seems impossible to persuade theatresports groups that even people who make the suggestions don't want to see them acted out. If you ask "Who are we? Where are we? What are we doing?" you may end up as two knights in armour tickling a nun who's swimming in a bowl of Jell-O. The audience will laugh at the suggestion, but many of them would pay money not to see that scene acted out. Suggestions allow improvisors to share the blame with the audience—"Yes we know it's crap, but it's the crap they asked for!" Or perhaps they want to make sure that nothing they care deeply about appears on the stage. If the ideas have to come from the performers, there's a risk that their inner demons may be revealed. Good! Great! But the average player doesn't want that.

These days I encourage storytelling, and I try to persuade players that getting suggestions ruins their work. I tell people that they should take risks and stop altering my games to make them safer, that "no risk equals no game." I try to explain that the spectators are as interested in players who fail as they are in players who succeed (so long as they stay good natured). Some groups remove the Warning For Boring so that scenes can stagger on interminably while the players search for a "laugh to end on." Some groups even remove the penalty basket (although how they absolve players who are obscene or racist I can't imagine). Some players have a really strange attitude. I heard one say, "Why should I care what the audience thinks? I'm a performer!"

The audience is what matters, not the performer. That's why it's wonderful if the players are humble. A player who is arrogant may be successful, but he/she has to work a lot harder. And why shouldn't players be humble? Inspiration is something that happens to you, something that you are open to, something you can accept—but it's really a gift from somewhere else. If a show goes well, you should be pleased, but you should give your thanks to the Great Moose (the muse of Loose Moose Theatre) rather then stroll about congratulating yourself. And if the show goes badly you shouldn't punish yourself.

Our real task is to reeducate people. Schools train us to be dull (i.e. to make safe choices). School is designed to produce obedient and negative people. Normal education is a branch of the military, quite clearly.

The Moose (Tony Totino) and Commentator John Gilchrist.
PHOTO: DEBORAH IOZZI

The Beginning Years of Theatresports

CAN YOU ALL SPEAK IN ONE VOICE?

The first theatresports teams were an assortment of personalities with little to connect them at first glance but a passion for improvisation. Consequently the first years of the game may be characterized as fractious and disorganized, but extremely passionate. In this chapter the players describe their impressions of how the game first looked and how it evolved into a highly competitive, though locally based, league.

Frank Totino

It's like years later you go back and you see these people that you were so involved with, and it's like family. It's not like people you used to work with, or even people you used to go to school with, or anything like that. It is *so weird*. There is some kind of connection between people. I've never experienced it in anything else. Except in family. It's like at some level you are interested to know what's on with everyone even if you don't deal with the people anymore or have much to do with them. You see them a couple of years later, and there is still . . . something. That's the really interesting aspect of it actually, how it pulled everybody together. Because I guess the act of improvising is like baring the bones as far as your ideas go. And you've allowed others, and they've allowed you. The only other guys who really get to do that, I think, are musicians, jazz musicians who have been into pure improvisation. And painters who are trying to break through somewhere, so they let it all fly.

24

I don't know. I guess each art form has that sense of where you've allowed yourself to be out of control or in the control of something else. That takes over and you become the spectator of your own actions. And I think that's what really interests people in art. It's not the fact that they come up with a nice picture at the end, although that's great, it's that there is something *there* afterwards.

Improvisation was always an interest of mine. I always used to do things, get involved in certain projects when I was, I don't know, fourteen or fifteen, and I never even thought of it as improvisation. Later on when I got involved in music, the idea of improvising, or jamming, was the most interesting to me.

Anyway, Tony [Frank's brother Tony Totino, also an improvisor] was going to university, and I went up there one day because, being a rock musician, I was broke, and it was the last day to apply as a student. I'd applied a couple of years before to go into marine biology, and they'd accepted me, but I never showed up. I think I got a gig or something. So had I showed up, I would have been in marine biology. I had to decide what I wanted to do, and I think I put down Fine Art on the thing.

I said to Tony, "Look, what's going on? You're in the Drama Department. Is there anything there?"

And he said, "Actually yeah. There's this guy named Keith Johnstone who seems pretty good. He's actually *done* something in theatre, as opposed to a bunch of guys who graduated with an MA [Master of Arts] and got a job teaching acting or whatever the hell." Which everybody else in the whole department was.

He said, "Yeah, Keith and his wife, Ingrid, are pretty neat. And they teach differently from everybody else."

I said, "Okay, fine. I'll try the Drama Department."

I went to the library and looked up a bunch of stuff, and there he [Keith Johnstone] was. So I thought, Well shit, maybe this guy does know something. I'll try it out. I don't have a job; I may as well be a student.

And I talked with him quite a bit too. He came over to my place one night, and I played a bunch of my improvised music, which is really weird shit. Then he started in on his improv technique, and I was sold.

No, I wasn't sold. I just bought it completely.

Speaking in one voice? L–R: Dave Duncan, Tony Totino, Kathleen Foreman, Frank Totino, Veena Sood. PHOTO: DEBORAH IOZZI

Mel Tonken

Okay, it was actually while I was doing my BFA [Bachelor of Fine Arts]. One of my instructors was Keith, and we were doing improvising in our acting classes, not much else. Keith got a group of his more talented students together to start improvising outside of school hours. Usually in his basement.

After a while it became pretty obvious that an audience was going to be a necessary component of this, and we just decided one day, why not start a theatre company? And we did, and that was the beginning of it. We performed in various places at the University [of Calgary], at SAIT [Southern Alberta Institute of Technology], I think at the Pumphouse [Theatre] and a few spots around town. That's how it started. There was myself. I'm not sure whether Veena [Sood] was in at the very beginning. I think she actually came later. There was Ingrid, Frank Totino, Ross Patton and Dennis [Cahill], yup.

Initially it was improvisation completely directed by Keith.

John Poulsen

If I can go back a bit, I remember even in our acting class, Johnstone was searching for something that would make theatre as exciting as sports. He would very often refer to theatre as being . . . standardized, regional theatre . . . as being somewhat dull, whereas sports were always exciting.

"Why is it"—I'm paraphrasing, but—"Why is it you can fill a sports arena with twenty thousand people, yet you can't fill a theatre with two hundred people?" And he would, even at that time, suggest that there was something about the competitive nature of it. That theatre could be and should be that exciting. I think even then he was struggling for it.

When I did the Secret Impro thing, I think he was trying to start up again what he did in England—the Theatre Machine. But I do believe that even at that point he had something, some idea of taking it further somehow.

Anyway, when I came back [from an extended trip to

Europe] I saw theatresports. It had been going on for, from what I heard, eight months-ish. When I saw it the first night, I thought, Um, this is very interesting. It was basically the theatre games we had done in Acting 300 and in the Secret Impro group put into a competitive format.

Johnstone was still very much the moderator, or the . . . what is a good name for him? Ringmaster, perhaps. The warm-ups were directed by him, and the warm-ups were *en masse*. All actors would participate. At that time, there were two teams, and I believe it was probably the Moosettes and the Moose teams playing. And they seemed pretty even at that point. Even though the scores may not have showed that, I felt the teams were very even.

Dennis Cahill

A roommate of mine in first-year university told me about Keith. He'd taken a class with Keith. Keith was here [the University of Calgary] and then went somewhere else to teach. This friend of mine said, "If he comes back, you should take a class with him." So the following year, Keith came back, and I thought, Oh, I should take a class with him. It was through Keith's class that I was turned on to the idea that you really could perform improvisation in front of an audience. I found it very exciting.

The following year Keith started something called the Secret Impro Show, which was a noon-hour improvisation show at the university, and it became a very exciting idea that you could improvise in front of any audience. I found that very appealing. I guess I got on with it well enough for Keith to ask me to participate. I suppose if it had been a real struggle—I mean, not that I thought we were very good. We have the original videotapes of the original Secret Impro Show—*really* dreadful. But on the other hand, we kept doing it, and Keith kept encouraging us, and I think it certainly kept me around. I suppose if Keith had slammed the door, I might be doing something else now—an accountant making huge sums of money.

Veena Sood

I'd always wanted to be an actor, well, since I was fourteen, and I could not stand the kind of acting I was seeing in the theatre scene, in my acting classes. I couldn't stand the kind of theatre I would see down at Theatre Calgary. There was something about the style of acting that I couldn't take. It was all this kind of thing where you didn't believe a word and it was . . . I hated it.

And then everybody was saying to me, "Take this Keith Johnstone guy's classes. It is so fun." So I took his classes, and he unlocked my entire life's repression by the culture I had been raised in and brought out this other side of me that obviously was screaming to get out, and he unlocked it very easily.

I loved the kind of people he was hanging out with. Like, I thought this Frank Totino guy was really cool. He seemed like a real hippie.

Tony Totino

I am currently living in Oslo, Norway, where I am working as an improvisation teacher, and I occasionally have the opportunity to direct a short play. Yeah, I've been here for about a year now and will be here for some time, I suppose. I first started with theatresports at the Loose Moose Theatre Company . . . I don't know . . . I guess it's almost fifteen years ago. I played in what I believe to be the first *ever* theatresports game, which was started as something of an exercise during what we called the Secret Impro Show at the University of Calgary. A bunch of us used to meet at the noon hour to present an improvisation show, or alternately, if no one showed up to watch us, we'd use it as a rehearsal session, and during one of these, we staged a show which was the basis of theatresports.

Boy, it was a long time ago.

As I recall, I was in the middle of the study of dance at the university, and Keith invited me to do the choreography on a play he was presenting, and the *kind* of rehearsals that we had during that play, the sort of work that he was doing was very, very interesting. The rehearsals were fun, whereas rehearsals for all the other plays I had worked on were pretty much like having root canal surgery—they were painful! They were long and boring, and, you know, you would sit for hours while the director droned on about where to stand and how to speak and, you know, which eyebrow to lift and things like this. And Keith's rehearsals were filled with excitement and fun and discovery.

So when Frank [Totino] suggested that I come along to Loose Moose rehearsals, I agreed instantly because I wanted to find a little more of that excitement that was certainly absent from other theatre things and *completely* absent from dance rehearsals and dance work. I never found that type of excitement in dance either.

The first couple of months of actually doing what we called theatresports, we never really mentioned it. It was just one of the exercises we'd work on during a rehearsal session. I seem to recall it [theatresports] would tend to take the form of something we would do at the end of a training session. We would loosely split up into a couple of teams, and we would play. Usually we would play the No Blocking rule. The first rule of theatresports was No Blocking. One team would take the stage until they had made a block, and the other team would challenge them. And if the challenge was upheld, then the other team would get an opportunity to play.

It went on like this until one day Keith suggested that it was interesting enough to try out in front of an audience, and we did. And . . . the audience went nuts!

Dennis Cahill

The Secret Impro group—it's very strange. It was very much that Keith said we were going to do this, and we'd just do it. It was like we were sheep. Keith would say when we were going to do a show, and we'd just do it, blindly. Like I said, if we had the videotapes now, we'd be very embarrassed and probably never go on stage again. We became a group of people who would follow Keith.

There was always that sort of "tag" put on those people who were with Keith and those people who were against Keith. We were the people, basically, that if he said something, we believed it.

Veena Sood

Keith phoned me up. . . . I was in his acting class. It was, I think, the 300 [senior] level. And he had decided that there was this magical combination of personalities in this particular acting class that he felt he could use to do some research in his work. So he decided to form a theatre company, so he phoned me, and I went to his house. And he and Mel Tonken had decided to form a theatre company. And they hadn't decided on a name, but the choices were Loose Moose or Sodom and Gomorrah.

He chose . . . I think he chose Loose Moose.

Dennis Cahill

You know, when I think about that group of people now, they were very, very different personalities, and for the first few months it just seemed to work by virtue of the fact that Keith would draft us and we'd go along. The personality conflicts started to come out later, after we'd gone on for four or five months. But I think it actually was a very diverse group of people. I think maybe at the time we could have said, "Oh yeah, we're all friends. We're all energetic." But now it seems to me that it was quite an odd group of people. You know, would you put Ross [Patton] and Mel [Tonken] and Frank [Totino] in the same room? These are not automatically people you would pick for the same group.

Frank Totino

Suddenly there was somebody putting into words the way you'd been thinking for years but couldn't explain to anybody.

You already know the idea, like when he started explaining Status. For years you would stand around parties in the kitchen and watch it happen. Guys with hats and blades and beer bottles, and how they would move. How somebody would walk into a room, and everybody would shift around and move. How people would do "this" in the ashtray [he mimes flicking off an ash], and suddenly everybody is flicking their ashes.

It was just, you had noticed stuff like that, but you never talked about it to people because if you did, they would look at you like you were nuts. Now you realize that you were nuts because you *didn't* talk about it. And everybody else was noticing it too because everybody who hears about it understands right away. It might piss them off, they might resist it, but they *know* it's true. They don't want to believe because it goes against your, well, it goes against your training. But I loved it, I thought it was great. Yeah, shit, I'll go along with whatever is happening.

He [Keith Johnstone] called me up at the end of August and said, "Look, Mel [Tonken] and I are putting together a theatre company, and we thought you might be part of it." Then he asked me to come over and talk to him, right? So I went over and had some tea and ate some biscuits, and we talked about the idea of putting this together. He explained, "We think we are going to try and book the Pumphouse [Theatre] on Sunday nights for a few months and see what happens. We'll meet here in the basement three nights a week and try to put together an impro group."

And I remember saying to him at the time, because I had been through several groups already, groups of people trying to perform in public, [like] music groups, and the idea of working in a group, I really liked. I liked the idea of sharing the ideas around because things develop so much faster that way.

Anyway, so I said to him, I said, "Sure, I'd love to join your group, but I only want to join on one condition, and that's either I'm in it all the way, or I'm not part of the group." You know, I wanted to be in a group that was truly a group and working as a group—not as part of a group of people that gets told [what to do], or working for somebody else or doing somebody else's idea . . . because, you know, working in groups—it can be pretty weird. Somebody takes over, and the next think you know, you're following orders. And that was just not what I was interested in.

Veena Sood

So anyway, he [Keith Johnstone] invited a few of us to his house one night. The people he invited were Mel Tonken, me, Frank Totino, Ross Patton, John Ghitan, Sandy Caroll and his [Keith's] wife, Ingrid. And Dennis [Cahill], that's right. So those were the seven. And we met, I think, once a week at Keith's house. We'd have a cup 'a tea, eat and go down into his basement. And he'd start teaching us the games.

A lot of the time, the games we were learning in his basement we wouldn't learn in acting class because they didn't apply to acting. Over time, he decided this was a good thing.

We started doing really good work. We started to do the Secret Impro Show at noon hour in the basement of Calgary Hall [at the University of Calgary]. And they started to sell out. Then he [Keith Johnstone] got word that the Pumphouse was available Sunday nights. So he got in touch with a stage manager, and he got a carpet, and that was about it. I don't even think we had a backstage thingy. There was some semblance of curtains on a rod. And that was our set. It started selling, and it became bigger and bigger, attracting all sorts of other people. It wasn't theatresports yet. Theatresports evolved out of that.

Rick Hilton

I remember taking a 200-level [junior] acting class with Keith that Jim Curry was in, and in one of those acting classes he [Keith Johnstone] started talking about these Sunday shows, and he was encouraging us to come down and watch. And he said that after a while they were getting kind of stuck. That they seemed to have reached a certain level, and it was hard for them to get past that.

Secretly I think that what he wanted to do more than anything was to introduce Jim Curry into the group. Because Jim was this fabulous improvisor in our class. The funniest man in existence, right? But Jim had told me that the couple of times he went into the basement of Keith's house to improvise, he got all this . . . "Fuck" and "Furthermore" and "By the way." A lot of real heavy status. And this sort of "Keep The Jim Curry Out" movement developed, right? And I think that Keith was struggling to find a method to introduce Jim into the group. And out of that sprang the idea of having teams. Like, there was obviously a competition between the new people and the old people.

Frank Totino

When we first met, there was Keith, and he was the Guru, but he wasn't The Boss, you know what I mean? In those days Keith never used to say, "I want. I want this and I want that." I don't know if he does anymore either. But he sure as hell didn't then. And that was a big, big step.

Nobody seemed to say, "I want to do this." Or, they *would* say, "I want to do this" . . . and then get up and *do* it. And everybody seemed to jive on that right in the beginning. The first little while. Either it was happening that way, or I was so naive or blinded that I didn't see it.

Things moved very quickly. By Christmastime, a couple of other people had started hanging around the group. Jim Curry used to come down. He was the assistant stage manager for a while, but he was also in Keith's acting class at the university. I think he was in a class with Rick [Hilton] and Kathleen [Foreman] and those guys, right?

Anyway, there were seven of us originally who liked to get on stage, and Keith used to pare it down to five. He used to put five on stage, and the other two would be assistants. So we changed, alternated back and forth, and—what the hell—there became a sort of competition in the group. To get on stage. Because everybody wanted to do everything all the time 'cuz we were young improvisors and were just discovering it all. We were ready to let her rip.

And so there was that kind of competition, which never used to bug me. It never used to bug me that other people wanted to get out there all the time. I thought that was the whole point. 'Cuz Keith used to say all the time that you should be *wanting* to get up and get out every time. And when you're told to sit down, you should be disappointed. And I was, you know. You would be disappointed for about a minute, but then it was okay. Life goes on.

Mel Tonken

I think, well, I think it was an original idea of Keith's, and then certain things kind of paved the way for it. We always had this envious fascination of how sporting events attract these humungous audiences, you know? Made us sick. How thousands of people would go to the football games and the hockey games, you know, and twelve people would come out and see some real talent. So there was the thing about making it more like a sporting event to attract a wider audience. And I think maybe there was . . . not competitiveness, but within the group, we liked to show each other what we could do and how talented we were. And the idea of having two teams was sort of born in that way.

Veena Sood

The point thing started coming from his acting class. He couldn't get people to remember to stand up straight, and he'd have to keep saying, "Stand up straight, and speak up!" And Keith got very agitated by having to keep reminding people, so he found out that if he awarded a prize, like points, to you at the end of a scene for being stronger voice-wise, or whatever, it would be all that people needed to remember to do all these things.

Rick Hilton

I remember clearly the very first game that was actually

played. And I think the only other person who is still playing is Tony [Totino]. It was a lunch hour where we had a group of improvisors, quite a huge group, and we were doing nothing but blocking. So that's when he said, "Let's separate the group, the room, into halves." And this half can improvise as long as they don't block, and if *you* see a block, you yell "Block!" and you rush on stage.

And when he saw the way the competition thing fit in so easily, I think *that* is when everything clicked together. He realized that he could make the present Loose Moose group a bit better. Bring Jim Curry, his protégé, on stream. And then all these other weird personalities could come and become involved in it.

And then we, the Moosettes and the Moose Team, started throwing in our sports expertise. On the judging, the penalties. I think that is how the game evolved in its early stages.

Veena Sood

It evolved from our work.

Rick Hilton

Definitely. He watched what was happening and then got the idea from that. There's no doubt in my mind.

Veena Sood

And then it just started to snowball. I remember the day I came in with a judge's outfit.

Rick Hilton

Remember all the different rules? Every week we would have a new rule of some sort. We'd try another variation.

Veena Sood

Can't do that, can't do this.

Rick Hilton

The judges scored by time. We had, you know, warnings, penalties—the rules just compounded. It was like this chemical that you throw a rod of electrically charged copper into, and it forms a crystal. Keith was the electrically charged copper. But it's really chicken and egg, you know. If it weren't for the chemical, would you have had the . . .

Veena Sood

Yeah, chicken and egg I think is a very good way to put it, because . . .

Rick Hilton

Because we needed Keith, and at the same time, when I look back on it, he needed us, and it was a real, it was a real . . . family. And that was the exciting point about it. That we had this guru, this guy, who was our dad, who had the family working well. We sought advice from him. We looked to him for guidance and support, and that was exciting as hell, it really was . . .

Veena Sood

And Keith, he bailed a lot of us acting students out of some troublesome times, being victims of bad acting teachers, and thank God for Keith at that time. So as soon as you find an acting teacher that you can trust, that you actually can see results from in your work, you glom onto him. We were doing things like taking trips to Banff together. Like, everything was together.

Rick Hilton

It was a real family, and it was an exciting time.

Veena Sood

There were lots of times that we just stumbled blindly and failed miserably and threw things out that weren't working. And this theatresports thing, it was like one day, it just went *bing!* We *all* have this *bing!* It was after one night at the Pumphouse, and Tim O'Leary was there, and the next day at school in the basement of Calgary Hall [at the University of Calgary] we were all walking around going, "Wow, would you imagine if we *did* this. Like, this could be big."

Rick Hilton

Yeah, it felt like we were in a group that was on the cutting edge of something really wonderful.

Veena Sood

Well, we were.

Rick Hilton

Yeah, I guess we were.

Frank Totino

I've tried to think of this so many times . . . when exactly we came up with the idea of doing it . . . but I know it was in the basement of Keith's one day. One evening. How the rehearsal used to go is, we would try out some of the methods. We would do Arms or Status Transfer or we'd do an I Love You or whatever, and then he said, "Let's go out and see who can do Status Competitions." That's what it was! See who could be the highest in Status, or the lowest, and then we came to the point one night where we said all right . . . and it may be Keith who said it, it probably *was* Keith who said, "All right, the guy who wins the Status Challenge gets to stay up." And somebody else comes in and does the Status on him, and we went on, and we started doing it like that. We found it interesting for one guy to stay up and hold the floor.

But then we soon ran out of stuff because basically Status was the only thing you could really directly call a competition. And *then* we started talking about, well, wouldn't it be great . . . Keith had always said wouldn't it be great if he could get theatre to be as popular as sports, you know, as football or wrestling and stuff like that—where [the audience would] come in great droves. They'd know how the game is played, they'd have their favourite stars, but they don't know when the Great Play is going to happen, so it's the spontaneity about sports that they really like.

We talked more and more about this. Talking about how the hell you would run a competition in theatre. You could do Status Challenges, sure, but what else? Well, let's see who can do the best Arms Expert. Things like that. And we started practicing these things down in the basement there.

And then Tony, one night, brought up the idea of giving scores, giving points or something. He said, "Let's keep track of the scores, and we'll have teams." How should we do that? We went through all these methods, and Tony being so . . . sort of like the *Encyclopedia Britannica* on feet, said "Why don't we do it like they do in skating. They hold up cards," you know. And it got to the point where everybody was doing all right.

Tony Totino

Well, I'm pretty certain you'll get lots of different stories about *how* collaborative the process was, but as I recall there was *nothing* in place about theatresports. Nothing at all, except perhaps the idea that you could have two teams vying for possession of the stage. That was the basic premise. I think every step along the way was, in fact, a collaborative idea.

Now, certainly on many of the points, Keith would suggest, "Oh well, we need to do this. It's too easy. . . . It's too simple to play a scene where you don't block," which was the first rule of theatresports, you know—No Blocking. Well, that became terribly easy for us—to get along with that rule. Then [came] the rule of Not Being Boring and then all the other rules. The Inaudibility Rule, which I reckon was quite funny, you know, if you couldn't be heard . . . I think that shows you how inexperienced everybody was at being on stage at that point.

All the points . . . you know, the judges—how the judges should score, penalties, sitting in the penalty bag, one minute or two minutes—all these different things—having a commentator. I recall all these things being kind of discussed on the moment. "Wait a minute. Do we have to have judges for this? Judges with score cards?"

I seem to recall being one of the first judges, myself at one of the first theatresports shows we did. I remember dressing up as a kind of blind man with a white stick, tapping my way out to the audience. Saying I'd call it as I saw it.

Dennis Cahill

[Talking about how the form of theatresports evolved] . . . Well, some of it was the technical aspect of actually putting on a sporting event in the theatre, and to some extent that's where some of the people with the sporting background—like when Tony [Totino] started coming. Tony the sports fanatic. Those people would automatically have ways of wanting to do this because "This is the way you do it in sports." I mean, when we first started doing the tournaments, you would automatically go to the sporting people for consultation. So there were those aspects that people had a say in.

And I guess the other aspect was how to make it work as a performance, and that would be more of Keith's input in terms of how you actually present improvisation in a competitive format and make it work. [Hence] the things like the horn calls or the initial format of theatresports, not blocking, how to reward people, how to get them off stage. Later, I think Keith's focus was on how to actually get the players to improve their improvisational skills and to look at the game for variety's sake. If you'd done one thing, try to do something totally different for variety.

That's what I remember—the technical how-to-actually-make-it-a-sporting-event. And also the artistic side of it—how-to-make-it-a-theatre-event.

Tim Lee

Well, I went to the University of Calgary, and I got into Johnstone's classes. I spent a lot of time in Johnstone's classes 'cause I was there. Then I missed my philosophy class after that a lot. Because I liked to hang around. And then, eventually Kathleen Foreman told me that I should go down to the Loose Moose Theatre, and I went. . . . Well, I thought they'd *invite* me into the theatre. But they didn't. They just suggested I go there and hang out. And I guess I did that.

When you did that, then you became part of the Company, although you didn't know. You were never really secure, since no one sent an invitation, which was pretty weird. Anyway, so that's what happened. That's how I got involved.

There was a dynamic to it that was kind of interesting. That is, you'd get to perform, and you'd get rewarded for things that you wouldn't get rewarded for anywhere else. Rewarded for acting up, rewarded for *getting* up—you'd get rewarded for all those things that you are trained *not* to do. You know, you'd get rewarded for these things that you have been holding back from doing.

Plus, I had no friends.

And the people involved seemed on the most part to have a common sensibility. I think there was a lot of . . . anger, you know. I think there were a lot of serious comedians, tremendously serious people who could be funny very quickly and easily, or witty, or had some sense of charm. Maybe timing.

I think that, by far, most of the people were tribal, and they all wanted to find a place in that tribe and be secure. They wanted a gang. I think most of the people were angry at society. . . .

It was a reaction against dullness. Against a dull theatre, as we saw it. You know, I had been in plays, and Tennessee Williams didn't do it for me. I didn't understand why all these plays were important. I can now look back and say "You know, I'm older, and I've got a degree, and I've got all this education, but I *still* don't like his plays." I mean, that's how Serious Theatre was.

And it was fun to be quicker than those guys were and to express our own values.

Mel Tonken

I didn't like theatresports. I played it for five years because I was part of it here at the beginning. There was a certain pressure there that I hated—the pressure to win, the pressure to excel, the pressure to be better than other people. To come up with other ideas. It really seemed to contradict the very nature of improvisation. I felt that strongly and eventually I stopped doing it.

Rick Hilton

It was pretty weird for me because I came from a completely nontheatre background. I was in the fourth year in university trying desperately to become a lawyer. I had been accepted already in several law schools, and I had no inclination to become an actor whatsoever. I had completed my entire degree, and my last year was filled with options, so I said I was going to take the easiest wankiest courses I could . . . which were always the drama classes, right? No essays; no exams.

Then I meet this guy, this teacher who has all these wonderful people, by coincidence, working with him. Looking back, I realize that probably the reason why I got hooked was because of Jim Curry, because he became such a good friend, and I love the man so much. He was such fun to be around, and then he and I were in this impro class together, and so it was just like this great friendship and this great art. The excitement of it. I think that is what really dragged me through the first four years . . . this euphoria around theatresports.

Frank Totino

Well, how do people get off the stage, you know? We came up with an idea—first one to Block loses the stage. So we got really good at No Blocking, at which point scenes would go on forever, and we'd never get thrown off the stage. They weren't very good scenes, but they wouldn't go off.

So over the course of the next six months, he [Keith] said, "I've got these guys in my class at university. There is a group up there, a bunch of them I think would make decent improvisors at some point. So why don't we arrange a . . . well, bring them down?"

So they came down. I think they came to a couple of rehearsals in the basement. And then he set up the first match in that second half of the first year of Loose Moose. Yeah, and the next year it became a main draw.

Rick Hilton

The first years, everyday we were finding new things. Every week. It was wonderful. I think it [the euphoric feeling] has lasted, even fourteen years later. So the combination of him [Jim Curry], Keith and the euphoria of the discovery, I think, is what has held me, even to this day. And now I feel . . . Christ—there is no goddamn way I'm going to get out of it. I'm going to stay no matter how poor I am. No matter how many times the audience boos, I'm going to hang in there because I am dying to know what is going to happen in ten and twenty years, you know?

Dave Duncan

In the old days of the Moosettes when, you know, it started . . . you would make a list of what you were going to do. You would do a Word At A Time, and then A Typing Scene and then a blabidy blab [Gibberish].

Then we progressed to the point where each individual on the team would have their own list. And you would have three or four things that you were going to set up, say two Challenges and two Freezings. And Jim Curry would have two, but he wouldn't tell you what his were, and you wouldn't tell him yours, so that every time that Jim would go up and set something up, it would totally surprise you.

It got to the point in the last few years that I played theatresports where we wouldn't even make up our own personal list. We would totally wing it off the bench. I guess that was our philosophy—always trying to surprise your teammates, always putting yourself at risk.

John Gilchrist

I graduated from the University of Calgary in 1977. I went off with another friend of mine to start a children's theatre company and work on that for a couple of years. At that time, I was living with Tony Totino up on Centre Street. And then we moved down to First Street—2325 – 1st Street S.E.—which became the official headquarters of Loose Moose for a short period of time. The official mailing address for Loose Moose, actually. A lot of people tended to live there—Dave Duncan, Dave Cameron. During that time, I went to various Loose Moose events and things, on the weekends, and I sort of watched the progression of it, and then in the spring of 1979, we decided to pack in the children's theatre company, and I came back to work full-time in Calgary.

I'd been back about twelve hours, and I got a call. Well, actually Tony told me that Mel [Tonken] wanted to see me. So I called Mel up and he asked me if I was doing anything and I said, "Well, not much for the last twelve hours," and he said, "How would you like to do some publicity, promotion, marketing and advertising stuff for Loose Moose?" I said, "Well, it sounds like an interesting idea. What's it pay?" And it was like a hundred dollars a month or something and I go, "Well fine. No problem. I'll just put in a thousand hours a week for that amount." I started working with the Moose June of 1979, and I stayed until July of 1984, so almost exactly five years.

I was never involved in the theatresports on stage except for one ill-fated evening, which shall forever live in infamy and only in my darkest dreams. Sometime around February 1980, Bob Percy came to me and said there was no general manager at the time. Even though I was doing PR and promotion, I ended up doing a lot of the administrative stuff because that had been my background, and I sort of said, "I have the time so I'll take care of them." Anyway, Bob Percy came to me and said, "As general manager of the Pumphouse, I've got an empty week in February. Would you like to fill in?" I said, "I'll talk to Keith about this and see what we can do." At that time, theatresports was really starting to take off. Theatresports itself had only sort of formalized into an idea over the summer of 1979, and there were starting to be teams and competition over that fall.

So I went to Keith and I said, "They've got a week. How about we do a tournament?" And he actually didn't think it was a very good idea at the time, which was not unusual for Keith. Most of the times, he didn't think any new idea was a good idea. He thought it would be kind of a pressure cooker. But he broached it with the group as a whole. And the idea perked up the imaginations, and after all it was the middle of February. It was pretty horrible out, and we decided that—what the hell—let's just try it.

So we had the first annual Calgary Invitational Theatresports Tournament for a week in February.

Frank Totino

The second year, I really started to think that it would work as a sport. I really expected this theatre company—because it was so neat, and the audiences were obviously seeing something and appreciating what was going on as much as we were—I really expected that we were going to do amazing things. You know. Do great! Build up and do plays, one acts and all that stuff. I really thought we were going to produce some amazing shit and get organized and become . . . a Great Theatre In Canadian History, you know? I really believed all that stuff.

And that's what I was working towards. I thought, I'll devote my entire energies to this. And I did. I was doing everything for it, everything, you know. Awake or at home, that's what I was doing it for. And [for] theatresports, when I started to think, to really look at it. I used to look at the audiences, and they used to *react* like sporting fans. I mean, we used to talk about it all the time.

You never saw people in plays leap to their feet and raise their hands over their heads and all roar in one voice. I never saw that in my life. The only place I ever saw that was at a football game when they scored.

That happened in theatresports. People would love something so well that they'd leap to their feet when a team won elegantly. If they won a challenge or something like that, and it was a great scene and it ended well, the audience would roar in appreciation of not just the guy winning but the whole thing, the appreciation of the interplay, the Act, right?

And I thought, Gee, I think that we've done what Keith used to want to see happen, to get audiences to respond like sports audiences.

Dave Duncan

I actually believe that sport and improvisation are really close together. In hockey, improvisation is going on all the time. The transition game from defence to offence is amazing improvisation—now, of course, they have scenarios set up so that once they get into a zone, they are going to try—especially on the power play. But going from defence to offence is an amazing transition, and it's all improvised. The amount of spontaneity that has to be involved for a football receiver to know when to make his cut, when to leave the ground, what foot to jump off to meet that ball in midair.

I mean, it's not thinking. It's reaction. Maybe it's instinct. It's being able to let your body and your mind take over without trying to force them into a certain thing. In the early days of Loose Moose, we experienced that on a weekly basis because the work back then was actually *discovering*.

John Gilchrist

It's interesting. When I was going to the old Impro Shows, they were a lot of fun. They were total chaos, you never really knew what was going to happen and every once in a while things would get going. Then Keith would stand up and start talking and bore everyone to tears. And I always thought, Keith should not be on stage; he should not be directing this because no one wants to watch a director. And Keith knows this himself. I mean, nobody pays to watch a director. People pay to watch a performance, and I remember having a conversation with Tony [Totino] in the spring of '77, saying, "You know, this is really interesting, but it doesn't go anywhere. It's not like watching a hockey game. When you watch a hockey game, you start somewhere, you watch the action, you are really excited and then it ends. And you go, 'Okay, I'm fulfilled.' But with an Impro Show, you're never really sure where it starts and finishes. It just sort of 'is,' and then it's ten o'clock and you go home." And both of us thought it would be a good idea if somehow sports could be incorporated into this.

Now, I don't think this was a unique idea. I think this was an idea that was sort of coming into its own at that time. People were thinking of putting impro into some sort of format, and God knows what other formats were thought of, but this sports one just seemed like a very logical one. Especially for a bunch of guys, predominately, who were used to a sporting format.

I think Keith understands wrestling and soccer sports formats, and I think he was the one who *wanted* to move it into a sports format. I know that the idea may have been his, but I think it was the environment of having an art form and having a whole bunch of creative people who didn't have a lot of restrictions on them but who did have the sports orientation to a certain extent.

Gary Campbell

I was in high school. I was taking a drama class in high school, probably would have been grade twelve, and the teacher there sent a group of us down to theatresports one week. And we approached someone who directed us to Keith. Said we really enjoyed it and were very interested in it. And I think it was at a point where they were sort of on a membership drive. This was '78 or '79. And Keith said that would be great. It was great that we were interested and wonderful and invited us to his home that week for a workshop. And he and Ingrid made supper for us, and we ate supper, and they discussed theatresports and improvising a little bit, then gave us a workshop. And we played our first game the next week. I think we played three weeks in a row. Three games. I was the only one that continued.

Jan Derbyshire

I was eighteen. I remember thinking it was really bizarre, like walking into a cult almost because everyone that was up there looked a little different.

It [theatresports] was at the Pumphouse doing well. Sunday nights, the Moose, the Moosettes and any new teams played. You started as a new team. And you had to play these *giants*, and you got waxed, you know, you got waxed like a hundred and ten to five. I got 'pied' for a year in a row, you know, like a pie in the face.

That was weird. That was the only thing that made me want to not keep doing it.

Bruce Hunter

Let's see. I guess the year I got involved with theatresports, I think, was '77 or '78. Pretty early, yeah. I guess I got involved when I was really young, seventeen or eighteen years old. I went with my brother. I think he drove me there or something. I was blown away. I thought it was great. I had to be involved because I thought it was so cool. It was something I had never seen before, and it was pretty much how I want to work. You know, pretty open and without scripts and . . . everything else was just too regimented. So it was a place to be able to do characters and stuff, jump around and scream and stuff. And that was something you couldn't do in school. That's why I was involved in drama. You've probably heard that a million times before. A lot of that time was quite a blur in my life. I can't remember a lot of the details, but I do remember after I saw it for the first time, I went back and stayed to talk to people so I could get involved in it.

I think that was right at the time that people were concerned about getting new teams happening. Keith was running workshops, and the people who were in the workshops were Jan Derbyshire and myself and Graham Davies and a few other people, and we eventually formed our own team. There were only four or five people in the whole class. There weren't many people involved. We were one of the new teams, or like, the *only* new team that was being worked on. That was "Bear Paws." I don't remember any other teams being organized at that point, and I was really quite surprised that there weren't more people playing, why there wasn't a lineup of people. But it seemed like a secret thing.

In the workshops . . . we did the exercises, and then Keith would say, "Um, ah, try this," you know? Or he would stop and go, "say this to so-and-so." And you would, and then you would start to see . . . although his way of workshopping was really quite unusual. Instead of giving you something and saying, "Go with it," he would stop it and say, "Do this." He would tell you how to improvise, you know? I thought, "This is sort of neat."

So when I walked out on stage, I didn't even know what we were doing. We were just waiting for Keith off to the side, saying, "Stop. . . . Do this. . . . Do that. . . ." So it was pretty new, but it was fun. I can't remember what happened. I think we lost quite a few times. I got 'pied,' so I guess it was around that time period, before they took the pies out.

Frank Totino

We started to draw people who didn't go to the theatre but who loved sports. So I think the competition between the teams was really important to those audiences at that time. I think that's what caused the competition amongst the teams to get so intense for such a long time, you know. And it really did. I mean, it was like—"Gotta win, gotta win. Win! We haven't won in weeks. I can't stand the pie in the face . . . " or whatever. There were so many reasons, but you had to win. I don't ever remember being rabidly *against* anybody else on the other teams. It never seemed to be personal to me.

I thought the competition amongst the teams was great, and I remember going into Keith's office one time in that year, in the second year of theatresports, and I said, "You know, Keith, I think we've really got something here that could take off. Like, if you got the idea, if you've got a league going where you *really* had a league . . . Let's say, for example, you had other cities doing it . . . but even if you just had a league in town here. It would become really popular, I think. If you could get it to the point where it was between cities, I think it could work like sports. Where people in those cities would actually be rooting for their home team and all that sort of stuff.

Mark McKinney

I heard about theatresports from Norm Hiscock. We were buddies from Newfoundland. We wanted to get into comedy.

We wanted to do something at the radio station out there, but nothing ever fit, you know. We needed a way in. We just finished taking a screenwriting workshop, and then a few weeks later, we were up at the Moose watching theatresports. Miraculous! I just knew I wanted to do it. The attraction was comedy. I didn't get into the actual impro until later. I didn't know that there was even impro happening. I thought it was comedy, but later on in Keith's acting classes in university, I understood it.

What makes it incredibly special is that it's a great ground base zero learning pool. If you can do impro, it gives you guts to go out and react. Plus, knowing what you're going to do requires the relaxation of a good actor and the timing of a comic. And you can do many other things. It leads to many things.

I'd love to play theatresports, you know, sometimes, but it's something you have to be around. I'm not sure I'd be good at it anymore. It's like, I don't know, ballet or skeet-shooting. You gotta keep your eye on it and do it well.

It's incredibly useful, yeah. It's sort of my whole basis for the way I approach performing—not so much theatresports itself, but I try and relax the same way. It's like Keith said: "Good acting is really improvisation at its best," which is probably the most solid and singular piece of advice I've kept around for performing.

I think Keith is probably the only genius I've ever met. No, I do. I think he's an extraordinary man.

I could go on about theatresports forever. I just found that at a certain point I believed in it religiously, and I finally got an inkling of what it was, you know. This is weird for me because when we were in the Audience Team in Calgary, I was doing characters and I was improvising, but I didn't know how to relax. I didn't know how to really improvise. It's something that made sense when I was in Toronto because suddenly I was seeing a lot of what wasn't impro. And it sort of drove me in the other direction to try and actually go out with nothing in my head and be reacting, you know, for that ten, fifteen seconds, to make scenes come completely alive. And for a while I was teaching it.

We all met through theatresports. Norm and I knew each other in Newfoundland. There we were in Calgary, hanging out, trying to find some way to do comedy, and then we went into theatresports, and the like-minded people seemed to be Frank Van Keeken, Bill Gemmel and Gary Campbell, and then Bruce McCullough showed up. We were all sort of comedy obsessives and wanted more to do than just play theatresports, so that's how Late Night Comedy evolved.

Yeah, Loose Moose was the only place to go. It really was. I don't think I could have gotten into performing any other way. I would have made a lousy stand-up, really half-rate. [Loose Moose] was absolutely perfect. It was a group of people who cared about something artistic, and Calgary was the only place to do it. It's sort of odd when I think how fluky it was.

Bruce McCullough

I actually remember the first time I went. I went and Tony Totino played. Then we went to 4th Street Rose [a local restaurant]—me and whoever I was with—to eat, and he [Tony] was there. I just remember the sense that he was this really big guy, you know. Like he was a big man on campus. I think I was a little attracted to him. Which is probably more of the uglier side of me.

It [the improvisation training system] was sort of like a farm system. If you looked good and didn't actually physically hurt someone on stage then . . . *you could play.* It was very gladiatorial in nature.

My first team was called Jerry's Kids with initially someone named Lars Lehman, who I've actually kept in contact with. He's sort of producing films or something in Alberta now. And Andrew Pearce. And another guy who is a friend of Andrew's, who I can't remember. I just remember that he was really tall. And he was only there for a couple of weeks.

There is something great about the first time you can hold an audience's attention and not quite understanding what that means and how you can lose it and all that stuff. Yeah, I actually remember if I had a good show, I would be happy for a week. And if I didn't have a good show, I wouldn't necessarily be unhappy for a week, but I would try not to think about it until I got the next chance. It would be like a starting pitcher who has, you know, had a bad game. All he is concentrating on is the next game.

John Gilchrist

It was fun! In my mind, I think of it as the Golden Age of Theatresports. After the 1980 tournament, people sort of jumped ahead a little bit. People would get more energized and pick up more ideas, and sometimes that adrenaline would help them create new things. After we left the university tournament in February of '80, throughout the rest of the season, before we moved to the Simplex, was great theatresports. The last four months or so were in the Pumphouse, and then that carried over.

When we moved to the Simplex, there were so many people, so many teams. The Gonzos, the Polanskis, the Audience, the Moosettes, the Moose, the Velvet Hammer, the Bull Moose, Mel's Angels. So many good, talented people. I think it sort of carried through until the summer of '83. That was the peak of it for me. I found that even though individually performers got better, and individually scenes got better, that after that time period, it didn't seem to advance as much.

Rick Hilton

It was a Golden Era of Theatresports. The Audience Team was playing.

Veena Sood

It was really hot.

Rick Hilton

We'd just moved into a new space. Even though it was a horribly located space, it was a great building, and crowds were coming out Saturday and Sunday.

Veena Sood

Yeah, yeah. Plus Late Nights were selling out.

Rick Hilton

Yeah. And then Keith started to pull back in the theatre.

Veena Sood

Right. He didn't show up for weeks at a time. And we weren't ready for that yet. So all of a sudden we started to fall apart.

Dennis Cahill

We moved into the Simplex, and because we had our own space, because we needed to do more, we took even more people, so there were even more teams, and also the teams that had been playing for a couple of years became settled, and the competition grew because of that to some degree. There was team pride, and there were teams that didn't like playing each other or resented playing each other. I remember the Audience Team causing some consternation among the players because they were always going out to break the rules.

The competition became very, very heavy at Loose Moose— to the point where there were yelling and screaming arguments at the meetings afterwards. I remember one particular evening I heard there was a threat of a fist fight, almost typically high school, in the parking lot after the show.

So the competition went way overboard, and also at the same time, other things began to happen. I think the players began to feel that perhaps they were being abused due to the fact that theatresports brought in a lot of money, and they weren't feeling like they were getting their return, and there was some resentment. I think this was the point where the Player's Association came in. The Black Days of Theatresports, as it's sometimes referred to now.

Tony Totino

Oh yeah, the . . . ill-fated Player's Union. This was about five months, I believe, after we, the theatre company, moved from performing at the Pumphouse into the Theatre Simplex by the airport where it's still located now.

The number of people who had joined up and had an interest in playing theatresports had boomed, had at least doubled since the time we had played at the Pumphouse. There was quite a big gang of people, but it seemed to us that there was also a big gang of people who were hanging around and were not training to learn theatresports and had no particular interest except in being on stage and showing their faces, and we thought that perhaps the time was right to form an association of players to train on our own and . . . the goals we had then are quite fuzzy in my memory. I think it had something to do with wanting to maintain a certain amount of control over who we had to play with.

I know Keith thinks we were trying to "usurp" control of theatresports from him, but I don't recall anyone actually suggesting such a thing. Nobody ever thought that. It never occurred to me. I know Keith thought this was an outrage. He was extremely irritated.

Frank Totino

It got weirder later on when we moved to the Simplex. The whole nature of the company shifted. See, I had really thrown my whole weight, all my weight into this thing. I used to have a studio, and I turned the studio over to the Company. I used to spend all my time doing stuff—when we moved to that complex up there, I think things changed then because they took that place with some kind of private deal. Without ever talking to somebody to say we've got this or we've got that. We all got into it full bore, but things changed then, and it was . . . I don't know. Within the next year or so you started to realize that you weren't a member of the Company. You were just a performer, you know. Suddenly this thing that you'd been spending three or four years at, which becomes a part of you, is no longer! You're part of it, but you have very little input in it, in terms of reality, because suddenly the numbers start to take over, right? And you've got what turned out to be the situation whereby Mel and Keith were the Company, period. Just the two of them.

We used to get into terrific heated arguments about what to do with the Company and . . . how to maintain its integrity because most of the people, I think, in the early days wanted the improvisation to evolve. You could see the tendency for it to become a yuk, yuk show, a show full of stupid jokes and gags, which was totally against the whole idea of concentrating on a spontaneous moment, you know. What you wind up concentrating on is making stupid gags. . . . It becomes a business because you can make a business out of gags.

That's what most of it has become as far as I can see. It remains popular as far as an audience draw goes. What it looks like to me now is the audiences seems to be within a certain age group. The audience doesn't grow. The only thing that gets older is the performers, the guys who stay in it.

Dennis Cahill

A number of the players felt that they were in need of some sort of association to uphold their rights, and this caused a lot of trouble. I think they didn't feel they were getting their due. I can't remember specifically what they wanted, but they wanted some power, some return for their work—whether that was monetary or in terms of direction of the company. Most of these were players that had been around for a couple of years, and eventually a Player's Association was formed. What I remember of it was that the committee [members] themselves were elected, and most of the people who had been voicing their opinions loudly were on the committee initially. It seems to me that over a period of a few weeks, the committee people were dropping out—like every week there was somebody dropping out and you had to replace them. I had always been against the committee, and it got to the point where I was on the committee because so many people had dropped out. Anyways, the committee died a horrible death.

I just didn't see the point to it. I've always been to some degree under the opinion that Keith basically, for all intents and purposes, created the idea of theatresports. There's always been some discussion—"Well, other people brought in other ideas"—but I think basically it was Keith's idea and also that Keith was always there for the company. And my feeling was that I appreciated the benefit of having worked with Keith and working with Loose Moose. To me, that was enough. I didn't really see a need to confront Keith or cause Keith problems or to upset him in anyway over something as simple as Who Has The Power or Who Doesn't. Did not concern me. I either tried to stay out of the arguments, or if I was in the arguments, I was more or less on Keith's side. The committee . . . never really came to anything, and Keith came back.

One of the stipulations of Keith coming back was that we would disband the teams, that we would no longer play with set teams—we would play with scratch teams [teams made up from players randomly collected for an evening's performance rather than teams that played together each week]. And then, this way, the competition would hopefully lessen. And the result of that was that the competition *did* lessen—it was not crazed on Sunday nights anymore. There might be arguments, but they were more personal arguments as opposed to team against team—and basically theatresports went on from there as far as Loose Moose was concerned.

Tony Totino

Ultimately the Player's Union was utterly ineffective. It had no effect whatsoever. Finally someone called a meeting just after a theatresports show, and Keith was there and he sort of read the riot act to us about the idea of a Player's Union. He said he'd have nothing to do with it, and it would have nothing to do with the Loose Moose Theatre Company either, kind of thing. He said this idea was out, forget it, there would be no more Player's Union, he didn't want it around and that was that. And from that point on nobody ever thought about it, so the Player's Union was kind of a thing stillborn.

Dennis Cahill

I don't know. The more you talk about it, the more you have to say. There was something that I was thinking about. This was something that I'm sure comes up in other groups too. When we first started playing theatresports, there was always some discussion of whether it was *theatre*sports or theatre*sports,* and I do remember having very vivid discussions about what was more important—the sporting aspect of the show or the theatre aspect. I think, ultimately for me, the theatre aspect is more important. The format you can fine-tune to some degree, but after that it doesn't matter if the improvisational work isn't of value. I remember that in earlier discussions, some people with a sporting background were quite adamant that the sporting aspect of it had to be very true to life, which inevitably would end up like a rule book with, like, one hundred and fifty pages, but fortunately that never came true.

Pattie Atfield (Stiles)

I came to theatresports through high school. When I graduated I went into the work experience program. I told them I was interested in theatre, and they placed me at Loose Moose. That was the end part of '83—yeah, fall of '83. So I was hanging around and heard about theatresports.

I remember so many Sunday nights—like, I wouldn't miss a

Sunday night, I was so faithful to being there—and being *amazed* by what was happening on stage. I started going to Sunday night classes.

I think you get caught up in it because you start doing it and you start learning it. What you're learning is so unique and makes so much sense that you keep doing it because you want to explore more and you want to learn more. I don't think it's a conscious "Oh, I'm succeeding, so therefore I'll continue." I think it's that you get wrapped up in the energy of it and the enthusiasm of it and what you are learning and the whole atmosphere of the Moose at that time because everybody was still around—the Vancouver expedition hadn't left yet. It was always learning, even when you were doing front of house you'd be learning because you'd be watching two of the improvisors goofing around with each other. The freedom, the excitement, the ability to do that, you know?

I never thought that I could and still don't think that I can—not to the level of the people who were there doing it before me. I think there's a real difference in levels of training, you know, because if you take the First Wave or the Beginning Group or the Creators or whatever, it seemed like everything in their lives was around theatresports and creating theatresports and developing theatresports. That's the way you viewed it and the way that you got into it. When I came along it was already there, so I had to learn what had been already done, but I didn't have to create it. So because I didn't have to create it, I haven't developed the skill that you have to use to create things.

I think it goes back to that creating situation because you've got the—I don't know—the seniors or the whatever you want to call them . . . you watch them play and the technique and so forth that goes into it is leaps and bounds above any of the other companies. You can just see it, the way that the mind works. I remember seeing a scene once where Tony was taking the skin off somebody, and he took it off them and realized that it was *inside out,* so he straightened it. That's so bizarre, but it makes so much sense. I never have seen that kind of quality in anybody else—in any of the other cities. So the technique—and I don't know if it's the creativity level or just the being used to it—I don't know what it is, but there is a real difference there.

The difference I find between myself and most of the performers in other cities is that I view myself as a very supportive improvisor because very seldom do I drive a scene or take over a scene. I tend to accept things immediately and go with whatever's going on. Not a lot of people are trained in doing that. When I was in Australia I had quite a few people say to me, "How do you just say yes to everything?" because they were all trying to drive the scene, and they were all trying to be that front-runner. Nobody gives in. But then, they probably don't have the confidence in people because they haven't had a group ahead of them that they watched. You know? Whereas, when I've watched you [Kathleen Foreman and Clem Martini] or Dennis [Cahill] I know that you guys are good, so I know that when I'm on stage with you that it'll work as long as I say yes and help out.

Rebecca Northan

My friend Christian was volunteering up at Loose Moose for a long time, and I'd been telling him that we were doing it [theatresports] in school, and he told me that Loose Moose was looking for high school teams to play in the ten-minute game and to phone Roman [Danylo]. So I did and that's how my high school team went up and played. I liked it, so I went to Dennis [Cahill] the next weekend and said, "I had a great time. Can I stay?" He said, "Yes, I don't have a problem with that, but if we find out you aren't making a valid contribution to the theatre we'll ask you to leave." I was really scared and I didn't talk to Dennis for four or five months after that. But, that's how I started off.

I consider theatresports as a kind of hobby, really. It's a place to start. It teaches you to think on your feet, and the improvisational training fits into the game format of theatresports.

I have a lot of friends who played theatresports in the good old days, and when I hear them talk about the way theatresports used to be I wish I had been around then—as opposed to now. I think that a lot of the people that are playing theatresports now are not playing it to practice improvising—they're playing it to be on stage and to goof off and to have people look at them. Even over the past year and a half, I think the quality of the show has declined because the people playing it are a lot younger and they don't seem as interested in improvisation as getting on stage—"I want my stage time. I want to make people laugh."

I think that because . . . the younger people look at the forty-minute players [more experienced improvisors playing in the longer forty-minute games] and see them getting the laughs, and they don't understand what's behind it. They see improvisation from a performance point of view instead of as an art form or whatever. They only see the surface of what's going on, and they think that's what's supposed to be happening.

Jan Derbyshire

Well, it's very bizarre to say, but I make my living making things up on the spot. I make my living pretending. I make my living playing. That's pretty hard for most people to swallow.

Sometimes I think, "Oh my God, how am I going to take care of myself?" Etcetera, etcetera, etcetera. "Is this really just a prolonged adolescence? Should I smarten up, you know, and become an English teacher? So that I can have some semblance of a life, or do I stop trying to give this gift back." Because it is a gift, you know? I think for a long time I tried to give it back— "Oh thanks. I'm glad I have this and I'm glad you brought it out, but here, you take it."

I'm part of a community. If you look, everybody's really progressed and seems to be finding their spot and doing what they want to do . . . and doing the Real Life thing. Some people are having kids now, etcetera, etcetera . . . but I think we are a group of adults . . . that have been given a gift of being allowed to still think like kids. Because we do! Like, if you talk to Rick

Hilton, or if you talk to Dennis [Cahill] and Deb [Iozzi], it's . . . it's this group of adults that I miss when I'm away. Especially because they knew me from being Nancy Naive to Freida Fuck-up to . . . ah . . . Weird Jan now, who's doing okay. People looking at you and going, "That's weird," and you're looking at them and going, "You're weird too." I believe, I believe in Tony's saying: "It's the only place a lot of us will every truly belong." You know?

John Gilchrist

To this day, if I looked and I added up my ten best evenings in the theatre either as an audience member or as a performer involved in theatre, probably six or eight of those would be theatresports.

Spreading Out a Word at a Time

THEATRESPORTS GROWS BEYOND CALGARY

In many ways the theatresports phenomenon stands on its own. No other major Canadian theatre movement chronicled has developed and travelled with the same rapidity. But this is only one part of the phenomenon. The other part is the manner in which theatresports has spread. In this, theatresports has been more sports than theatre. Rather than waiting for individual theatre producers to bring a show or troupe to town, a group of eager young players has more often migrated, started training with locals and then applied for a "franchise" to play.

Keith Johnstone

I think theatresports spreads everywhere because people respond to its "looseness." I've always fought to keep theatresports open—available to anyone. And I resist rules that say what kinds of challenges you can make and so on.

When theatresports is captured by actors, they almost always isolate it from the community, but I prefer it when there's a mix of actors and "real people." Theatresports is so exhilarating to actors who are used to being treated as other people's dominoes that they want to close it in around them, and this can seriously hinder its spread.

It's not easy to keep things "loose." The culture has ways of doing things which seem intelligent, but they just create more of the same. Improvisation almost died out in this culture, and the "right way" is part of what helped to stamp it out. So I think the concept of "looseness" is important, not just on the stage, but in the way each group organizes itself.

At Loose Moose we don't even know how many people are in the Company. We know who's on the phone list, but we're not sure who gets on it—whoever's around when a new phone list is made up, I suppose. You can be in the audience one week and on the stage the next. I may not have a high opinion of some improvisors, but that doesn't mean that they can't get stage time. The team captains choose the players each week, and the team captains keep rotating.

A characteristic of Loose Moose is that the person at the top is not trying to force his views and wishes on other people. And yet, mysteriously, it often does express my views and wishes.

Dennis Cahill

I guess the next big thing in the chronology would be having Vancouver play. Keith had taken it [theatresports] to Denmark to play—probably in the spring of '78. He was teaching in Denmark every spring at that time, and so he introduced it to the Danes. Of course, we didn't have very much contact with them. As a matter of fact, we didn't have *any* contact with them.

He [Keith Johnstone] also went out and did workshops in Vancouver. I think it was late '78 perhaps or late '79 or sometime within a year or two of it starting here. I think they invited us for a tournament first. So the whole idea of intercity competition began with Calgary and Vancouver. Then we had a return tournament where they came out and played, and I guess to some degree it sparked the idea that you could have teams within a city but also have *other* teams—never dreaming that fifteen years later it would be played in fifty-odd cities around the world.

Tony Totino

In terms of the development of theatresports, I would say that one of the big events that made theatresports blossom as a phenomenon was the time that the Loose Moose Theatre Company, six or seven of us, travelled to Vancouver to play theatresports at Citystage against the people who were starting theatresports there. They had been doing it for a few months, perhaps three or four months, as a performance at Citystage. They would present it at eleven o'clock at night after the shows that had already been presented. So this weekend we had been invited out to take part in the first ever intercity theatresports tournament. Up until that point, it had been a local phenomenon here in Calgary, and again another minor, local phenomenon in Vancouver. After we did the theatresports tourney together, the combined effect pushed it into a different category. Now people all over the place had heard about it.

EDMONTON

Cathleen Rootsart

Edmonton theatresports began in 1981. I believe it began at Theatre Network, which in Edmonton is a company that produces only new Alberta work. So it fit into their mandate. The artistic director was Stephen Heatley, and he started something called Dark Monday, which [meant that] people could come and do whatever they wanted. I saw k.d. lang crawl across the stage in a garbage bag.

Theatresports began playing Sunday nights. I was in high school, and I actually saw the very first performance of theatresports in Edmonton in 1981. My high school teacher was teaching theatresports at the time. I think she was a little ahead of her time, and she took us down. From there, I started going to the workshops and got involved quite quickly.

I remember one of the first times that I played. My grandparents came into town, and they wanted to see this little hobby of mine, so I took them to this dark, dingy theatre. I'm playing a hat game with somebody who I have never seen since, and I made a classic impro error. He's standing in front of me just swaying back and forth, hunched over, and I said,

"What are you looking at?"—classic error—and he said, "Your tits!" in front of my grandparents!

I'm certainly the longest playing person in Edmonton. It's funny how impro just never gets out of your system, you know? Like, it's like a drug. Go to see an improv show, and you just wanna do it, right?

Wes Borg

I was fifteen. It was in a high school tournament, and I'd never seen theatresports. I did a workshop, and then we went up and did it. It was such a buzz, and we won the tournament. It was such a hoot, I just couldn't believe it. So I just never stopped.

Joe Bird

I played for about two years when I was fifteen, sixteen. Being up on stage was always an attraction. Being able to go for it, say what was on your mind. Then I recently started up again, and over the last few months, I've started to play a lot. I realized what I was missing. It's helped my writing because it definitely makes me not expect so much out of myself. As soon as I drop any expectations that I have of myself, it's just a free-for-all on stage, and that's a great time.

Neil Grahn

I had a great drama teacher in Red Deer [Alberta]—Steven Carney—who was really into theatresports. That's where I first learned it, and then I took acting from Keith at U of C [University of Calgary].

I actually started playing theatresports in Toronto. I played one match in Calgary. I was on a team where we were all new, and everyone else on my team was afraid to get on the stage, so I would. I got zeroes three times in a row, and the only thing I remember is the third time I got zeroed, I just fell to the stage [floor] and then crawled off from the middle of the stage. I felt good doing that. That was the only time I played theatresports before I went to Toronto.

I remember watching Dennis [Cahill] and Rick [Hilton] doing a scene, and there's one point where Rick said, "Hey, let's go sleigh riding!" and Dennis went, "Okay, here's the sled," and they got right on the sled. I thought, Oh yeah. I was just going way too slow. I can get this.

If I had stayed in Calgary, I would have come back to Loose Moose. In Toronto, there were times when I bombed, but I was pretty confident and things were steadily moving on. I moved in with Gary Campbell. They were doing the Audience team thing with Bruce [McCullough] and Mark [McKinney], and the *Kids in the Hall* was formed. I guess they deemed me good enough to play with them, and I regularly played with them, which was great for me. It helped my improvising so much, playing with these other people.

Just from travelling around Canada, I think everyone that does theatresports is separate from the acting community— except maybe Vancouver where there seem to be people who do theatresports who also do film and television. In Toronto, it seems to be more just who's ever out there jobbing actors, or anyone really. If you're a good improvisor, you're probably going to be a good actor, and also if you're a good actor, I think you can be a good improvisor. But among lots of performers [the feeling is] "Theatresports is okay, you know. It's fun, under-lined . . . I'm looking down my nose when I say 'fun.'" I run into that quite a bit.

Wes Borg

I can understand if you're an actor who spends days and hours getting every monologue down perfectly and knowing exactly what you're going to do every moment of a play. I can understand how theatresports would be blasphemy . . . "How dare you just go out there and knock down everything and do whatever!" I can understand how they get pissed off about it, but at the same time, you know, loosen up!

. . . I don't think you can slowly, painstakingly build a creative thought or a creative thing. Actual creativity is instant.

I think if you're a good improvisor, you're gonna be a good writer. I think it promotes writing far more than it does acting. I think a lot of writers would make good actors. I think that whole thing is holistic.

I had this thought last week and I have to say it until I get sick of it—I think that theatresports is a colonic, a creative colonic, a creative enema, yeah, yeah, totally, totally. Because if I haven't been writing for a long time, and I go Friday night and do theatresports, I just come out with tons of stuff. Some of it's crap and some of it isn't, but it just flushes you out so that when you do start to get ideas that you have to write down, you don't put too much importance on them, and you just have a lot and anything can work. That's the way I think it is.

I think if you become a professional, if you decide, "I'm going to do comedy," then I think it's pretty insane to not do something that's free, that's good exercise, that you learn from and that you get an audience for. Theatresports is the same rush you get when you're writing, the same rush you get when you're performing something for the first time, and it's both at once. When I'm writing a scene, my heart's pumping and I know exactly what I want, moment by moment. And when I first perform something, I get that too—when the audience understands it too. But in theatresports when you get both at once, it's incredible. It's great; it's really cool.

Joe Bird

It's happening right then, and you're not even thinking about it.

Neil Grahn

I think it's like tumbling headlong and really enjoying it—

not being completely in control but having a slight say in the control.

Wes Borg

Like being one of the runners on a bobsled. And if you wipe out, it still is a spectacular explosion, usually.

Neil Grahn

You think you're doomed and everybody in the whole place thinks you're doomed and no matter what you do you can't get out of it. Then someone will say something, and you'll pick up on it. It'll be like getting the spark in this blizzard and getting a fire going—"Whoa, how'd that happen?"

Wes Borg

Theatresports audiences are not a theatre audience! They're a movie audience.

Joe Bird

They're a video game audience.

Wes Borg

And different cities have different audiences too.

Cathleen Rootsart

Keith has never really been interested in Edmonton, frankly. We invited him up for workshops on numerous occasions, and

I can understand that going up to Edmonton isn't considered glamorous. I mean, we've always had to come to him, and we made the trek a couple times. And there was a bit of a disdain for that whole sort of "Keith's School" kind of thing for a while. So it was interesting when I went to New York, and *Impro* [*Impro: Improvisation and the Theatre*, Keith Johnstone, 1979] was their bible.

Wes Borg

I think the hypocrisy of theatresports is the competition. The place where that's most clear is in the way that high schools teach it. Then they make it a sporting event in the Alberta Winter Games. In the middle of these incredibly competitive athletic games, you've got theatresports, which is fake competition. It has to be fake. It can't be real, but all the people doing it take it seriously. It's crap, it's bullshit. Theatresports is like professional wrestling. It's not a real competition, but that's what makes the audience on the edge of their seats and up on their feet. You can't teach the idea to let go, unblock and be creative and then in the same breath say, "We're going to have a competition of this," because it's hypocritical. It's unfair. That's why I think theatresports should move towards big long narratives and towards being an impro show and not competitive. There are people in the audience who do pick up on it and realize that it's fake competition, but a lot of them don't and I think that's a shame.

Cathleen Rootsart

I think that Edmonton has a very physical style—high energy. I'm an anti-competitive person, and Edmonton is an anti-competitive league. Very often people will jump into each other's scenes from opposite teams and stuff like that. There's actually something that people in Seattle call the Edmonton Cross—someone comes into a scene, adds something quickly and leaves. If you were in a meadow tending sheep, a herd of sheep from the other team will cross the stage. I don't know if anybody ever knows what the score is at the end of the night. We play scratch teams. I think the last time that Edmonton had set teams was in '84 or '85. So a lot of the players that we have now never knew that theatresports was competitive.

Joe Bird

It was always the competition that had me on edge—frightened, basically, to be on stage in an improvised situation. Then at the Fringe Festival in Winnipeg there were a bunch of different companies, and someone decided to put on an improvised show. Just scenes, no competition. The stage manager was running around saying, "Okay, you two go out and do a scene next." It was brilliant. There was no pressure at all. I felt absolutely none.

Wes Borg

I think theatresports should always be a revolution of sorts—where people come and break the routines that other people find. Anything that shakes up reality is good.

TORONTO

Aubrey Pancer

I'm a chartered accountant by profession. My partner and I had an area of specialty in the Arts. My accounting office was doing work for people like Dan Hill and Murray McLaughlin and [Bruce] Cockburn and various and sundry celebrities. I was out at the theatre with my wife one night, and she picked up a brochure on some improvisation classes offered by Rob Salem, who was then one of the entertainment editors for the *Toronto Star*. It ran in four week cycles. I went down to Rob Salem's classes on Monday nights, and after about four weeks with him, it was like a repeat; you could do it again. So I did it again and I really loved it.

Anyway, to make a long story short, Rob Salem discovered theatresports in Toronto in about 1981, I think. A couple of people had seen it in Calgary, or Waterloo, and were doing it halftime at the Adelaide Street Theatre. They found a location called the Toronto Free Theatre. And on Sunday nights they started doing theatresports—a fellow named John Ferguson, Rob Nickerson, and, ah . . . the core group of guys that are now with the Frantics. Anyways, after it had been on a couple of weeks in Toronto, I went down to take a look at it, and I really fell in love with it. It was just exactly what I was looking for, and they had workshops. I got together a nucleus of about ten or twelve of us. They had already formed a little core group of artistic director and manager and whatever. And because I was an accountant, I stepped in and took over the responsibility of finance.

And that was about ten years ago. I had a really good core group of people, not necessarily professional actors but people who had an interest. It fulfilled a need for me personally. I workshopped a couple of nights a week. I really got into it. I played on teams on a regular basis every second week over the years.

I've always been a ham. I've always been a jokester. I do twenty different dialects. I've always been the class clown, but, you know, when you get on stage in front of an audience and you ask them for a suggestion, your heart goes a mile a minute. It is better than sex. Ah, when it works it's great. It really puts you on your toes. I've always been an improvisor. I've always been a bullshitter—in my business you have to be. . . . So it was natural for me and I had a lot of fun.

It [Toronto theatresports] is, as I say, nonprofit. We make no money at all. If my wife and former accounting partner ever found how much money it would cost me out-of-pocket to support this thing, they would both divorce me. I don't say it to pat myself on the back, but if I wasn't around, this thing would have folded years ago. The frustrating thing about it is you are dealing with young people, a lot of whom have no responsibility, who want to come on stage and have fun. And because it's a charitable organization, because it is nonprofit and they don't get paid, they don't have the same attitude towards it, perhaps, that I do. You know, I run the theatresports office out of my house. I would say in any given week, I probably spend between twelve to twenty hours, which is a lot of time considering the responsibilities I have. And sometimes it is disheartening. Sometimes you look at it and say, "What the hell for?"

The problem that I have here is the Catch 22. You need dollars and cents to keep it going. You need to advertise. But these people [theatresports participants] aren't hungry. They don't understand that theatresports offers them an opportunity. They can do workshop schools. There are government grants. If they go out and market and publicize it, you can bring it up to some level where I can pay people. I would love nothing better than to do what they do in Calgary where you've got people who are involved in the theatre, you know, because you've got a theatre in Calgary. It's a lot easier to work with. I am here one night a week, fifty-two weeks a year for the last ten years. Two free workshops upstairs every Monday and Tuesday night. That's our mandate—to spread, you know, spread the word. And it kills me when I work at our theatre . . . I get seventy or eighty people. It is not enough to keep it going. Eventually what is going to happen is if the people don't, if the base group—you know, the so-called administrative, financial, nonartistic types who understand it—don't keep coming along then it will fall by the wayside.

Listen, I have a current problem right now. In Calgary, they are basically identifying that Keith has a trademark on theatresports, and although it was discussed many years ago, nobody ever made money on it. This isn't for making money. So you've got Dennis [Cahill] and ah . . . Dennis organizing this thing and trying to expand it, etcetera. I don't have the resources to pay them, so I've got a problem. You know, I incorporated this ten years ago. I've got people coming after me, saying to me, we need to get a royalty on what you do here. And I'm saying to them, "Your royalty, where is it going to come from?" Last year I took in fifty grand, and I paid out fifty grand. Where would they propose that the royalty comes from is my problem. If they want to come here and organize it and do things to boost it based on their experience, I'd love to have them. They can share in whatever there is left because I don't want it. It's theirs to have.

Paul Bernardo

Aubrey is the singular reason why there is theatresports here, and at some point that should be acknowledged, even if we only have that sentence. Ian Chapman, John Ferguson, Aubrey Pancer. John Ferguson was the first, and Chapman was around for I guess the first five years.

I started in 1981 shortly after they had started. Next to Aubrey, I don't know who the most senior person is now because I have taken some people with me. [Paul is referring to a schism in the Toronto theatresports world. He left and took some theatresports players with him to form Big City Impro.]

My background is very different from a lot of people. I've been in business, sales and went into marketing in the mid-seventies when theatresports was beginning in Calgary. I always had a creative interest and started writing for a national firm. When I was in New York—I was tracking some material down because I also have to travel down there for my day job business—I met Sherry Flanagan with *National Lampoon,* and she was asking about impro. A guy from Second City, his name was Marty Feldman, was doing improvisation workshops at the Improv Club in New York. So I went to see him, and he told me that Paul Sills was in Toronto doing a workshop, and if I went in and mentioned that Marty said to let me in, he would. I did and I got in, and I did a workshop at Second City. In that workshop at Second City, I met all these people who had just started this thing called theatresports. I went down—they had just gotten into Harbour Front—and I saw it and got hooked on it, and, as is the case down here, began to hang around a lot, as you do, and you chat with people, and you let it be known that you are interested in helping out. I went there in September, and I performed for the first time just prior to Christmas in a ten-minute game.

Moira Dumphey

They started it in Toronto with a small group of people. They were actually performing it in a lobby in Toronto Free Theatre, and then in the summer, they moved it to Harbour Front. And that summer is when I started watching games, and within half a year, I started the workshops. So I was in within that first year.

That first year, an incredible amount of energy was given off by the performers because they were incredibly excited about it. They were thinking up new ideas, and it was like next week somebody might have had an amazing idea and actually brought in props. We had one guy who had an idea how to do an impro and narrative—like a typewriter except he is doing it as a storyboard . . . created a big pink eraser and a big pencil. And drew the props, drew the people in or erased them as he told the story, as the audience told them what they wanted. So people were just really thinking up new ideas, excited by it. And that is what I was seeing.

VANCOUVER

Jim McLarty

Now my understanding is that Keith taught a workshop, which led to the first performance in Vancouver at the Waterfront Theatre on Granville Island. Whether that was Day One here or not, I don't know. Somehow Ray Michal from City Stage got involved. Whether Keith came to him or he went to Keith, I don't know. It depends on who you talk to and who you believe. But it was suggested that it be done as a late-night activity at City Stage. So Ray somehow got the actors to play theatresports on a regular basis.

Vancouver Theatresports. Top to bottom: Rod Crawford, Lori Dungey, Richard Side, Jim McLarty, Gary Jones, Denny Williams. PHOTO: IAN FORSYTH

They started out by hauling people in off the street. They used to go to McDonalds next door and ask people to come in from there. They just said, "There's going to be a free show." And it caught on, you know. It has always survived here on word of mouth. We have never had to publicize it in a big way. In the early days, they passed the hat when the show was over to cover their expenses. By the time I got involved, it was already selling out. I think the price was three dollars.

I was a serious actor. I trained as an actor in Toronto, and I'd done plays and film work and stuff there. I came out here . . . because the film industry was starting to happen, and I felt that I needed a change. This was in 1980. I started by taking a few courses with other professional actors. I was taking a Shakespeare workshop with a guy named Bob Baker, and we'd go out for drinks after, and everyone kept talking about theatresports. Robin Mossley was in the workshop, and he was playing theatresports. It piqued my interest, although I didn't rush off to see it. I guess I was a bit of a snob, you know, because in those days I just thought that improvisation was a means to an end for a performer, not an end result. Why I felt that, I don't know. I totally don't believe it now. Finally I went down to see theatresports at City Stage, and it was great. For me, it was the first truly suspenseful theatre I'd seen in a long time because you didn't know what was going to happen next. I think we've all had that sensation during a film or a play where . . . you just know somehow what's going to happen, and you're not going to be surprised. The evening can be a bit deadening.

With theatresports you never knew what was going to happen next. Yeah, there's a bad scene coming, there's a good scene. I was amazed at the agility of the players. I saw some top people. Gordy White was playing. Barbara Russell, Stephen Dimopoulos, Robin Mossley, Bing Jensen—a lot of people who are either still involved or have gone on to unique careers for themselves as performers in this area. I was blown away and terrified because I knew that I had to check it out. I had to find out if I could do it, and I was really terrified that I wouldn't be any good.

The original idea was that there would never be a profit.

Whatever profit was made each month was returned to the performers. . . .

From the start here, it did attract a large number of professionals. And continues to, sort of. Now though, it's such a particular skill. Back in those days, I think it was more wide open and failure was more acceptable. But now it's really hard to fail. And I think it is really hard for new people. I don't know what it is like in Calgary, but we have a real hard time allowing people to develop and go through the experience that I described to you. I was given a lot of chances. And admittedly I survived because of my determination and because of a certain ability. But now it is tough for people to hang in long enough to find their feet.

I think Calgary has been more open to altering the rules as they've gone along. We haven't done that a lot. We've been truer to the idea that it is a sporting event, and the rules remain intact though we've played with them in small ways. I have been impressed with the way that Calgary will just throw everything out and try something new. I like the six-minute match, you know. I think that's exciting.

We always had a thing with the zero [refers to the zero or Warning for Boring, which a judge may give a team]. I've never enjoyed that. Maybe because I never worked with it over a long enough period. And it never took off here. We tried it once over a one-month period, and the audience were literally screaming for it to be taken away, they hated it so much. Whether that was because it really didn't work or because somehow we weren't doing it in the best possible way, I don't know. I also had a bad experience where a team I was on lost a tournament when the final scene of the event was zeroed—and it was a scene that should have scored quite well. We have gone instead with the Red Flag, which is thrown on by the ref, and it means that you need an ending so please find it. If you start exceeding thirty-second allotments of time, you start losing points. What we like about this is that it means that you started the scene and you end it. So the responsibility remains with the performers.

We need to look at theatresports because ten years is a long time to be doing something, and we've been doing it largely the same way.

[Vancouver theatresports was, at the time of this interview, going through negotiations with Keith Johnstone over the copyright. We asked Jim about this. . . .] Well, what is my comment there? We have a lot of respect for Keith. But we have developed on our own here. We haven't had a lot of input from him. I'm one of the people who believe that we owe him something. But even considering the fact that I've been around from a very early time, my contact with Keith has been very, very limited. We just want to find the level that we consider fair I think. You know, the last time we discussed it, there was a unanimous vote to counteroffer in a certain way, and the feeling was that we owed something to Keith, but that what he was asking was more than they were prepared to give. And we have a lot of people from Calgary out here now—I think at least ten. These people voted exactly the same way, and they have a much stronger history with Keith than someone like me.

Speaking in Gibberish

THEATRESPORTS GOES WORLDWIDE

One theory of linguistics holds that originally there was only one language, a Mother Language, which evolved in one location. Slowly that Mother Language spread from one continent to another, changing as it travelled, separating by stages into new accents, new dialects, related languages and finally into entirely new and largely unrelated languages. If this theory is true, then perhaps we witness in the worldwide progression of theatresports a similar process. Theatresports has travelled from continent to continent, but in its travels it has mutated, taking on distinct national flavours and idioms, sometimes posing the question: Are these new teams playing the same game . . . or are new games evolving?

THE UNITED STATES

WASHINGTON

Carol Douglas

I'm from Washington, DC. Theatresports is currently run by a company called W.I.T., which I founded. The acronym stands for Washington Improvisational Theatre. We fortunately licensed through theatresports. Unfortunately, well, unfortunately or fortunately, we split recently because some people wanted to do more—what?—basically more polished, safer shows. They wanted to try and make it professional and do some scripted stuff too.

We are now about six or eight [performers], and we have been performing weekly during the season in a really bad neighbourhood. There were a lot of murders, literally, and people selling crack on the steps of the theatre, and we don't want to subject ourselves or our audience to that. Space is a horrible problem. I'm sure this is a continuing theme. We find that churches are the unsung heroes of the arts in DC.

It all started very humbly and slowly in the spring of '86. I found out about it when I was living in Connecticut from Gloria Maddox.

I had been involved in some regular sort of semiprofessional productions and was in between shows, and I was looking for another group to think about joining. So I went to an evening of basically community theatre as it turns out. And it was dismal. It was grim! I was sitting there just sighing as all these guys plodded through their memorized lines, and I kept thinking, I can't stand it anymore; I'm going to go. Then I kept thinking, No really . . . a little moral support. I'll just sit it out.

And then . . . this thing called the New York Team of Theatresports, which is now Theatresports New York—these ten people bounced on stage with this incredible vitality. This blast of energy. [She remembers thinking] What the Hell is theatresports? Are they gonna play tennis or something? But they were wonderful. I was transfixed.

They continued to play there over the summer, and I went to every show, and then I saw an ad in a newspaper—a lot of serendipity is connected with this—this newspaper I never read, a tiny community newspaper called the *Shoreline Times*. Gloria Maddox had placed an ad to form this company, and it said, "Members wanted for improv company" or something like that. And I went. I did a small, unfortunately very short amount of training for a few months, then moved down to Washington. I arrived expecting to find a company to join and didn't. So I . . . took a big gulp, saw an ad for a trade show put on by the Actor's Centre at the Convention Centre, drew up some little flyers, got some balloons together, and I sat there with a little notepad, taking names of people who would be interested.

Since I really didn't know what I was doing, I just started

giving workshops. I didn't even call them classes. There was a lot of turnover. Then after a few months, the turnover stopped. We worked together with another company that had done improv before but had become sort of moribund. They got re-interested, got interested in theatresports, and we put on some shows together. We started performing.

NEW YORK

George Babiak

I got involved three years ago. I went away to a theatre conference, and the woman who was the artistic director of theatresports at that time came to this conference and taught a little workshop in improv. It culminated in a theatresports match for those of us in the workshop. And it captured my interest. When I came back to New York, I thought I could get into it and started taking classes with Laura Livingston, who is the current artistic director there. That's how it started. I got hooked.

Seeing the show made me think that it was less based on being a star and more grounded in telling stories, which is something I have always liked. I have seen plenty of improv groups in New York, and they are all . . . most of them do a type of show that is a simulation of a slick Broadway review. They are pretending that they are making up a review on the spot. And everyone in it is a great singer and a great comic. But not all of them are great at telling stories. They are all great individuals. They are stunning, charismatic individuals that can push forward their identity very well.

In theatresports, it seemed like they were slightly different. Not that the members there are short on charisma, but they would seem to cooperate more despite the competition aspect of it.

Up until last year, I think we were playing pretty much the standard Canadian games, the standard Challenge Match. And last summer we went to Australia. They play a very strict, structured type of theatresports, as you probably know. We didn't like a lot of what we saw, but we did like certain things about it—namely, the Australians were very capable of putting on a very good-looking show, which we felt we needed to do in New York. Our shows are a little too slipshod to attract people. So we started using bits of the Australian format. We did use time limits for some of the challenges for the first half of the show. For the second half, we didn't have time to fill in. We did use a game board, which we changed. It wasn't always the same game board. The Australians usually kept it the same all the time. But we like the opportunity for open challenges too, so we hybridized the show somewhere between Canadian and Australian—a little tighter than the Canadian but not quite as rigid as the Australian.

I don't know what we'll do this year. I think we will probably do more challenges because the company has been itching at the time limits.

SEATTLE

Randy Dixon

I'm currently the artistic director of theatresports in Seattle. I was always interested in theatre. Trite as it may sound, I was the kid in the neighbourhood who put on the show in the back yard, you know?

When I was fifteen or sixteen, I'd taken an improv class. It was awful, but I decided to give it another shot about a year later. So I called Roberta McGuire, who was in Seattle and who used to work for Second City. She knew Keith really well too. This was 1982, '83. I took a couple of classes with her, and it was in the second or third class that we started to do this thing called theatresports. I had never seen it, but I was intrigued by it. I wanted to get more.

I went to a party and there was this gentleman named Rich Hawkins whose name had been mentioned with regard to theatresports. So I went up to him at this party and introduced myself. He said, "Oh yeah, Roberta's been talking about you.

Wanna play on Monday?" So I ended up playing theatresports before I ever saw it, before I even knew what it was.

I thought it was great. I got bitten. The addiction, yeah. There are so many attractions for me. I firmly believe that if you can improvise, you can get on the stage naked and do something that's entertaining. Later, when you have a script, you can make it more interesting, and you are that much more comfortable on stage.

New York Theatresports. L–R: Dan Diggles, Laura Livingston, George Babiak, Sam Cohen. PHOTO: DAN LENORE

All my life I've been addicted to stories. I look at a scene like a puzzle, a story puzzle, something that needs to be figured out. I think it is incredibly challenging. In Seattle our focus has always been on the story. Don't go for the gag; go for the story.

Right now we are performing two days a week. For a long time we were doing theatresports both days, but now on the Friday night, it's theatresports, and on Saturdays, we do something else. Right now we're doing a soap opera, a continuing improvised soap opera.

We [also] have an outreach program, which goes into the schools teaching improv. For theatresports classes, anybody can sign up. They are six or seven weeks long, and we have beginning, intermediate and advanced. We have a lot of people who aren't interested in playing. They're just interested in learning for fun.

I have taken every workshop ever offered by Keith in Seattle, and I've been to Calgary and worked with him three times, including the International Impro School. So I think I've had quite a bit of exposure to his work. I think it's great! The thing that initially struck me is that the stuff Keith is saying is not necessarily just applicable to improv. I think it is a way of life, a thinking philosophy. That sounds sort of cultish and strange, but it's true. I've found that using some of those same principles in my life has helped me a lot.

I don't know if you've noticed this, but there is an incredible number of recovering Catholics who do improv. Isn't that strange? I've always wondered about it. Maybe we're rebelling against our youth or the things we didn't like about our youth. So many improvisors talk about being Catholic, talk about Catholic feelings. When I was a kid, I was this obedient little Catholic kid. But I was always sitting there thinking, This doesn't work for me, you know? It was so restrictive.

I think the challenge of improv and the challenge of spontaneity in general is if you are doing it well, you are teaching your brain to operate at maximum level. You are utilizing your brain to write, act and direct all in the same moment. It's like a muscle; you're using your brain muscle. It really gets you into active thinking. One of the things you train yourself to do as an improvisor is to use your brain in maximum overdrive while making it look completely natural.

SAN FRANCISCO

Rebecca Stockley

I was an actress, and I was living and working in Seattle. I met three different people that I knew, all at three different times, and they all mentioned theatresports. They didn't even know each other. I was doing the actor thing, and when you get together or run into each other, you say, "So what are you doing?" and all three of them said they were doing theatresports. So I finally decided I'd check it out. I saw a show, went to a workshop and got on stage within the course of a week.

When I looked at the stage and I saw how much fun people were having, that was the main thing. The group of people seemed very accessible. One of the things that bothers me about theatre, professional theatre, is that it's a closed world. It's very difficult to break into it, and this group of people that was doing theatresports in Seattle looked incredibly accessible to me. I came to a workshop, and the next night I was on stage.

I'd done improv comedy in the bar scene in San Francisco briefly, and I never, never really felt like I knew what I was doing. It always felt like every once in a while I would magically be hysterically funny, and the rest of the time I felt like a fish out of water. In theatresports, there are techniques for teaching improv that make it okay to be a fish out of water. It makes it okay if you fail. The other thing is that you learn to succeed more of the time. The accident factor lessens.

I had lived and worked in San Francisco for a few years and then returned to Seattle. And I already had a lot of friends in San Francisco. It occurred to me that a lot of people that I know in San Francisco would enjoy theatresports. I looked into it, and in fact, I had a newsletter from Loose Moose with a list of all the theatresports companies that you guys [the Loose Moose

Theatre Company] knew of at the time, and there was a San Francisco listing, a Bay Area listing, with Peter Coyote as a contact person. So I researched that a little bit and found out that Keith had been here several times and had done workshops with the Buddhist Centre. I contacted the people that I knew in that community, and there had been some workshops, but performances had never really gotten off the ground. I heard through the grapevine that there were a couple of guys from Vancouver that were doing theatresports in a church basement in the Haight District, so I got in touch with them and asked them if they knew who handled it. They gave me a defunct phone number, and try as I might, I wasn't able to find out who those fellows were.

So I decided that I could just, you know, start from scratch. I got in touch with a performance group called Fratelli Bologna. They're the Bologna brothers. They started out doing *commedia dell'arte*, and they perform their own material. I had dinner with William Hall. He's one of the Bolognas, and he asked me what I was doing in Seattle. I started playing one of Keith's impro games with him—the one where he tells the person that he has a story in mind, and then they ask him questions about the story. And he answers them yes or no. I got William to tell a story, and of course he thought I had the story in mind and that he was guessing what it was. He couldn't imagine how he figured out my story, so I told him what the game was and told him about *Impro: Improvisation and the Theatre* [Keith Johnstone, 1979]. The next day he bought himself a copy and fell in love with it.

He started working, doing some of the exercises from the book with the Bolognas. A few months after that, I did an all-day workshop with the Bolognas. Several months later, in November of '86, they got me down to do a month-long workshop with enough performers to do a whole match, and then at the end of that match, we did a mini-tournament where we brought a team down from Seattle. It was November '86 when we finally did a workshop that resulted in a performance, and some members of that workshop are still involved in theatresports now.

I gave them all the information on how to contact the Loose Moose and how to get licensed and encouraged them to bring Keith down to do workshops. So Keith came to see them do a show, and his notes were very harsh and they took them to heart. Several months later, I came down to see theatresports. It was very different from Seattle, and it was good. It had its own personality. In a way, San Francisco's theatresports is closer to Calgary's than Seattle. Seattle's changed too since then, but their show style was very similar to Vancouver's. San Francisco's tried to maintain a pretty strong link with the Moose and wants to keep growing, you know?

We play on Mondays because it's a dark night [most theatres are closed on Mondays], and the bulk of our twenty-one-member company that are active right now are professional actors. So we've explored doing shows on weekends, and our audience has gotten bigger when we've done shows on weekends, but we lose some of our performers, so we've gone back to Mondays.

Our theatresports format is sort of the West Coast format. Two teams play each other for an entire half of a show, which is forty-five minutes to an hour. We usually give a judge's challenge to start out, and then the teams challenge each other. We do it in categories most of the time, where Team A would challenge Team B to a justification scene or a storytelling scene or something like that. Then each of them does a scene in that category, and it gets scored by the judges. Our judges are players or one judge is a celebrity judge or an audience member is the entertainment judge. We try to honk scenes before they get the score down to a one.

What we're doing a lot this year is King of the Hill where we have two teams playing the first half and the winning team goes on to play another team in the second half and then the winning team goes on to play the next Monday. We find the audience likes to come back and see the team that won the week before. So it's good for audience development.

We've got at least one a month of what we call Long Forms. The first show in '93 is an improvised two-hour musical where we improvise the songs, we improvise the stories, the characters—you know, everything comes up from the title. It's something we've been working on for several years, and we made a lot of mistakes in the beginning, like introducing too many plot elements or too many story lines and losing control. And it got to the point a few times where the only thing that could happen is a mass murder where everyone dies in slow motion at the end because you can't possibly tie up all the plot lines.

We've [also] got *film noir* where the lighting is sort of dim, and there's some sort of mystery going on. We're trying screwball comedy again, you know, the really wacky, zany, thirties and forties style of comedy with broad characters and people jumping out of windows and that sort of thing.

We're [also] doing a space opera where the effects are done by improvisors on stage using toys and things as models.

We've got a space that's just for our workshops, so we've got an extensive adult education programme going on where, for six weeks, a student learns the lingo and does the really basic exercises. One night a week. We call that Improv One. Then they go on to Improv Two, and in Improv Two they start learning how to play the game. And if they pass Improv Two, they do Improv Three, and Improv Three ends in a workshop performance. So it takes about three months to get through that and get on stage, which would make people crazy in Calgary where they can get on stage right away. Then once people are workshop players, we have a new programme called The Institute where it's six weeks of working on a style of improv with the different coaches that can have specialties in that area. We're doing Shakespeare in January, and then in February they'll do a showcase where the students who take that class will showcase and improvise a "Shakespeare" play.

I administrate the high school programme, which is just beginning to grow. We've got Theatresports Weeks going on in the high schools in the Bay Area. We just did a workshop with six high schools that got together and workshopped all day and then did a tournament in the afternoon.

I really like theatresports happening in the theatre. I'm not one of the people that is hopeful that we'll be on national television. There are quite a few people now that have done theatresports that are on national television, but I'm not sure that that's the best place for improvisation. It loses its freshness and immediacy. The television audience does not feel like they're a part of the show. When you're in the theatre, the audience is just pulled onto the stage as though they are a part of the show. Their suggestion is used, they see the actors taking risks and they become a part of the risk that's taken and a part of the failure and a part of the excitement. I haven't seen that translate to video screen.

While there are a tremendous amount of talented people that are doing theatresports, one of the strengths is that it is in the theatre and in each community. It's a place where people can go and be a part of an event that's taking place that has goodwill and benevolence. We have less and less in our society where people can gather and just share their energy. We no longer go around the campfire and tell stories, and very few people go to church or whatever it is that brings a community of people together. That's one of the things that we're missing as cities grow larger, as the world grows smaller [through] communication—a place for people to actually gather and share human energy.

So a theatresports team in every city provides people with a place to go and experience being human. We need a "Fool" so desperately. There's so much fear. One of the things that's pervasive in the city streets is fear. So to see improvisors get on stage . . . obviously they're scared. The adrenaline's pumping through their bodies, they're doing things they've never done before—they should be scared. They do them anyway, and then if they fail, they survive and they bounce around like idiots and they goof off and it's just contagious and we need it. We desperately need it in our society.

LOS ANGELES

Ellen Idelson

Right now I'm the co-artistic director of Los Angeles Theatresports. I'm also the co-founder with Dan O'Connor. We were both members of Bay Area Theatresports. Then we moved down to Los Angeles. That was in November of '88, I think. Once we got there, we talked about it and decided what this town needed was theatresports. It's such a competitive environment . . . not very nurturing. The focus is to get involved in something that will get you involved in something else. Everything is a means to an end. You are always looking for vehicles to get you into the movies or whatever.

There are very few places you can just go and play, just for the sake of playing. It's turned out that theatresports is a kind of oasis in Los Angeles. It's the only place I know of that people can come and play in a low-pressure environment and not worry about who is out there, who's going to see them, what it means for their career.

I got involved in theatresports in San Francisco. They were doing a theatresports show at the New Vaudeville Festival, and I was asked to perform. The first time, you know, I was really frightened. I have always been so afraid of improv. I love acting, I love scripts, but I was deathly afraid of being out there and not knowing what I was going to do. Then I saw the joy that people had while they were doing it, and I thought this looks like too much fun.

We got all our information from Deb Weller in San Francisco. She was such a big help. We set out to mirror everything they did. When we got things going in Los Angeles, Barbara Scott and Ray Chase came down for our first intensive weekend workshop. All day Saturday, all day Sunday, and then on Monday, we did our first show. It all started from that.

We knew that things would happen and stuff would change—just by virtue of being in the city of Los Angeles. There are so many improv groups there. Tons. For that reason alone, I don't think we'll ever get as big as San Francisco.

Our company is still very young, at the beginning mostly run by Dan and I, and then we got a six-person advisory board. Now it's spread to the membership, and basically everyone has a job. We have a real good group in Los Angeles. It attracts a certain breed, and the people who can't hang with it are gone. I feel we are like a family. They are open and willing; they have fear, but it's not so great that it keeps them from making fools of themselves. That just makes them more fun to be with, more playful, more willing to experience life. And goofy—they are really goofy.

We do a lot of musicals in LA. We always finish our show with a musical, and we've sort of gotten ourselves into a rut because now the audience expects it. We've just started Friday Late Night shows where the first half is theatresports and the second half is Free Impro. We do a twenty-minute soap opera and a twenty-minute musical.

I've been travelling for a year now with theatresports. I went to the Fringe Festival in Edmonton in August, the Toronto Comedy Summit in April, the American Improv Festival in New York and now here I am in Calgary for the International Impro School.

I was really not intending to be this involved in theatresports. I was going to do it as a sideline and pursue my acting career as my main focus. But I was finding that I was getting really depressed about it and discouraged. Finding agents and stuff like that was really getting me down. Then I would go and play theatresports on Monday night and have such a good time. I find that the more involved I am in theatresports, the happier I am, the more relaxed I am about my career and about everything.

What I get from regular theatre that I don't get from theatresports is the opportunity to develop a character. To live with that character, breathe with it , get into the language and live with it for six weeks or whatever. In theatresports, I love to play characters, but they're so short-lived. I'd like to work on something that lets a character recur in different situations, like Dennis [Cahill] does with his mask character, Spaghetti. The thing I get from theatresports that I don't get from acting is the opportunity to make it up, be anything, any creature in my head.

Dan O'Connor

Our venue in LA is Theatre Theatre, which is a small seventy-seat house right in the middle of Hollywood. It's an old silent movie theatre, and we have the Big Russian Brewery nearby, so as every good theatre does, we have a good bar to go to.

Our company is about seventy people right now, a good

forty of them rookies. Lots of actors, some writers and a few just doing it as a sideline. If a rookie can do one of our outreach shows, they can pretty much do anything—a baptism by fire type of thing.

We used to do a workshop every month, do an introductory weekend and then throw them into the rookie ranks. But as we got bigger, we realized that we had people who were learning the same game for the fifth time, so it wasn't really fair.

Now we're running a school alongside of the company and as people leave, new ones who've shown some aptitude move in. For us, a good company member is someone who's *not* there to showcase themselves. We get a lot of people who want to go "Me, me, me." They're not there to have fun or be part of the ensemble. Even if they are brilliant as an improvisor, if they're an asshole as a human being, they're not going to be someone that we want in the company.

Unfortunately we're very white bread. In fact, we were talking to a couple of television people the other night, and they were very concerned that we were so white. If somebody is talented and ethnic, they're going to get a lot of work—is that a racist remark? I'm not sure. But it seems to be the case that all the talented Black improvisors we've come in contact with are working somewhere. We have a few people of colour working with us right now. It's hard in LA if people have their own gig. I know a couple of Black improv groups in south-central LA, and they are doing really well. Why should they come to theatresports and learn a whole new system? We haven't been able to solve this one, and we don't want to get into a thing of inviting in people of colour when we already have someone that's been around a while. It gets very touchy.

ORLANDO

Clare Sera

I'm from Vancouver, Canada, and I discovered theatresports there and was so hooked that I was completely addicted from the first match I saw. I went to the next workshop and then started improvising with the Vancouver company. Then a year later at EXPO '86, I hooked up with SAK Theatre, which is based in Orlando, Florida, and started working with them. I married one of the members. SAK does a lot of half-improvised story-telling so the members were very familiar with improv. The minute I got to Orlando, I wanted to start a theatresports league because I missed it so much. I missed doing it. There were a lot of women in SAK, but I was the only one who was comfortable doing improv.

It's funny because they're great performers, and they'll improvise within a structure they feel safe in. Like, the story has a beginning, middle and end, and any improvising you do is just icing on the cake, but when it came down to actually creat-ing a story they were terrified.

We started talking about theatresports, and in February [1990] we were given a space by the city for very cheap rent. It's right downtown and we turned it into a theatre space. It's SAK's first public performance space. We usually get hired by Disney or IBM, and all the performing happens under their name. So we started investigating and becoming part of the league. There's no competition element in Orlando. There's only eight regular players and six rookies that have been coming to work-shops and are working their way in.

We just scramble teams all the time, so there really isn't much competition. We did go through a phase where the points started becoming important to the teams, which seemed really silly when it was the same eight people night after night. But we nipped it in the bud fairly soon. We play theatresports on Thursdays at 8:30 and Fridays and Saturdays at 11:00. Orlando has nothing, and we didn't know if we would be accepted or not, but the people have been lining up. I think it might be fun to experiment with other forms of improv as well. Our main goal is to stay one step ahead of Comedy Sports, which is only two blocks away from us.

I feel that this whole theatresports thing is like a blessing on life. It's helped everyday living. It's such a great confidence builder and helps you to accept failure as part of life. I love the change that it has made in our company. We've nowhere to go but up, and we want to have an international tournament next April. Theatresports is like a healthy way to live—no blocking, no driving.

AUSTRALIA

Lyn Pierse

I wanted to be an actress but didn't think that I'd be able to. I thought I better have something else up my sleeve. In the early seventies, educational drama was really on the move, and this guy, Ron Danielson, who was head of this [drama] course, came to Calgary on sabbatical because Calgary was a centre for children's theatre with . . . Joyce Doolittle? Mr. Danielson saw this guy, David Lander, and said, "Come to Australia and organize things!"

In my second year [1974], when it came to electives, I decided I wanted to do this thing called improvisation. I had no idea what it was; I just knew I had to do it. Nine hours a week of this incredible work. Offers, yielding, no blocking, extending, small noses, big noses, full masks, half masks. Toured on a Victorian Arts Council Tour, went into schools as a team of eight and taught it. We were phenomenal, and we were absolutely trained in the Keith Johnstone method.

Then I ended up at NIDA, the National Institute of Dramatic Arts. They say fifteen hundred audition and twenty-two get in. There was such a gap for me between text and improvisation. I'd get a piece of text and a voice inside me would be saying, Advance, advance, advance! So I came right out into the industry, and I signed a big contract with the state theatre company. I did that for a long time—radio, feature film and stuff—and then . . . my luck ran out. I was, as we say in Australia, down on my luck. I couldn't get a job. I went back to Sydney and heard that theatresports had started and thought, What? What is that?

So I get to the theatre, and all these people from the industry were there because the theatre was going to be sold or pulled down. A person called Christine Westwood and her friend Sue Hill decided to get together a thousand people from the industry, and if we all put five hundred dollars in, we would all have five hundred thousand dollars, and we could buy this place, the Belvoir Theatre! So from Mel Gibson to every single agent in the country, film producers, casting agents and actors bought a whole share, half a share, a quarter, a tenth. We saved the theatre!

At the same time, Nonnie Hazelhurst, an actress, and Ray Lawrence, a director, came to Canada and saw theatresports in Toronto [1983]. They brought it back and said, "Look, this is a great way to make money for the theatre!" From somewhere they got the rules; we don't know from where. I've been told it was Vancouver, but the Vancouver people say they're not their rules. And the Toronto people say they're not their rules. Now I don't know whose rules they are.

We got a list of rules, a list of twenty-seven games, and we got these . . . commandments. And a guy called Denis Watkins put it into the format for production. We had eight teams on a night—compere, musician. . . . So there were thirty-six people on stage and three judges. The entire Australian industry was at these games. It was a huge event [June 1985].

I had THIS training and I'm watching these people improvise and thought, I know all of these games; I've been taught them! So I started to make suggestions, and they said, "Show us how to play it." I became the teacher. I knew all about it; I was taught it all those moons ago. And it had come back to me at a time when I was down on my luck. Somebody said, "Why don't you teach?" The spirit in me came back after all those years. I just wanted to improvise.

There were fabulous teams that came up. The first few weeks while I watched superstars make dingoes of themselves, you know, they loved it because someone very famous had just done something hilarious. At the theatre, we play on the sets for other shows so the other show comes down and in comes theatresports. And it is fantastic! The mainstage show was supposed to be the one that's fabulous, but it's theatresports that was booking out. It was unreal. But it did lapse off. And then it started to get a bit serious because there was going to be this big final, and the winner was coming to Canada to EXPO '86!

We had to win our state tournament. There was no doubt in my mind that our team was going to Canada. So all these teams arrive for the state final, and of course it's Tournament Torture City! And, well, there was no one to tell us what Tournament Torture was.

It was so competitive. You lose all compassion for the people you love, who you work with, who you have gone to heaven and back with on stage, who you thought you knew inside out. And nobody, nobody knew that. Nobody knew what the stakes were. We won that national tournament by one point. We were on our home turf, and it was impossible for anyone else to win. . . . That was the first rift between Melbourne and Sydney.

We were the Australian representatives to EXPO—the first Australian team to go, and it was a really big deal. We got to Vancouver, and of course they were in the middle of EXPO, and none of those players had any time to spend with us. Keith Johnstone wasn't there, and nobody cared how we played. And we played completely different from anybody else. But we beat Vancouver. And we beat New York. We beat England. We just won, won, won.

And then . . . the rough business. The British team disputed one of our marks, and the judges took it off; and then we were equal in points with them. It was an international incident. We remained very ladylike about it, but we didn't like it. And we became more and more tense. I lost that team, they lost me, we lost our spontaneity, we lost our creativity, we had no one there to coach us, no one to take us through the rest of the term as a team. And I was the person who said, "Stick with me kid, and you'll win diamonds." We had got there, and I couldn't take them any further. We got our certificate and everybody clapped. None of the Australians were on that stage except for me. They all left. It was awful.

I had to go back and share a house with one of the players. We would not speak of EXPO for three years, and one day he said to me, "When are you going to stop all of this? Lyn, it is nothing more than a game. It's a bit of junk."

I turned down work left, right and centre to continue this work. My agent has been in absolute despair with me. What happened after I was at EXPO was I set off with this $3,565.00 dollar grant given by the Australian Council. I went to every theatresports place right across Canada. I came to visit Keith. Sometimes I feel I can say things to him that are totally out of the blue that I know he knows. He just knows things, and I feel like I've told him things about me and my work that only he can understand. And I love that. Before I left, I told him about concerns that I had about Australian theatresports and how it wasn't getting the teaching that it needed or support that it needed or the artistic direction. I got everything I wanted from him and went back home and started teaching.

Next I went to New Zealand [1987]. . . . I knew the skills had to come first. I had to teach the games because the games are the preparation for theatresports. I had to give them as much as I could about how to keep the process going, as well as doing theatresports. I taught them the Australian method because that was the only method that I knew.

After Canada, I went home and said, "There's going to be another theatresports in Brisbane at EXPO '88, and I want to be the artistic director of it. I've just been to an international tournament, and it wasn't good, what happened in Vancouver. It did not celebrate the different cultural aspects of theatresports. And nobody should have to go through what my team went through again." If people were coming to Australia, I wanted to try to present something that celebrated the cultural difference. So I haggled my way into that position and planned it for two years.

Because we were in New South Wales trying to get this thing ready in Brisbane, there was a lot wrong with that tournament. We got a theatre that we couldn't manage because I wasn't there when the theatre was chosen. So we had a coliseum, an orchestra concert hall. Two thousand something seats. There were fifty-seven people coming from around the world, and I found out four days before they arrived that there weren't even any blankets in their rooms. I was a nervous wreck.

What we did was we played the Swedish Cup one night, the

Danish Cup the next. Each nation brought a Cup with them. Somehow all organizing came together, and the parts fitted into this mess. We played and every country's Cup went to another country. It was the only way I could work it for Australians to experience the rest of the world artistically. I was able to get the whole fraternity here. So while there was a lot wrong with that tournament, it blew the crack pot open. All of a sudden, all of the places that had been part of the Belvoir Street Theatre franchise, like New Zealand, didn't want anything to do with Australia again. There was North America! They could completely risk their own culture—deny their own livelihood and go into a style of play because, for no other reason, it wasn't anything to do with Australia. So they became incredibly international.

[Because the Australian Game is such a different permutation, we asked the Australian players to comment a little on the nature of their game.] In Australia, what happens is that two teams come up and they toss, call heads or tails, and if they win it, they get to choose off the One Minute Game board. They get to say who goes first. At that time, the timekeeper hands a stick back to the compere, and the compere says, "Death in a minute. Within a minute a situation is given, and within a minute someone must be dead. Your situation is a Laundromat." The team says whether or not they want a time-out, the compere has a chat with the audience, the whistle blows, on they come. They can have a halfway call if they like. They finish the first scene, and then it's scored. And it just goes on and on all night.

It is the magic formula! It's it! It's what brings them back. There is nothing sloppy about it. You never get that stuff you get up here [in Canada]. All that screaming on the bench and players fighting over what's going on. I'd nail them for that. The audience doesn't come to see that. They come to see the stage work. They want production. That's what the Australian game has—this incredible format. Put this formula on it, and stick it in an eight-hundred-seat theatre. The Melbourians played in their second week to eight hundred seats. It's a really big style.

SYDNEY

Marko Mustac

The thing is, they can't afford to pay more than eight people, and they don't want to give everybody a small amount. It's politics; it's bizarre. Once a week and it's packed, but it's not enough to support the performers. People are used to coming to see lots of teams. This year it has dropped down to four teams, and it will probably drop down again.

Sydney is not run by the performers at all. It is owned by a theatre who appoints someone to administrate and who tries to liaise with the players. But they work for the theatre rather than for the performers. It makes for a different kind of improvisation because it means you are trying to satisfy the box office. Theatresports has been in a crisis. Two years ago the theatre was saying, "Your audiences are no longer one hundred per cent; they are eighty-five per cent. You fix it up or the show is off." So suddenly there was serious work to make it more commercial. It's those kind of people who change the show. It's not controlled by the performers.

There are so many people that play theatresports in Sydney—there are tons.

[The nature of Aussie rules . . .] We had an interesting conversation at the Brisbane International. That was the one place where the difference in styles between Sydney and Canada really showed up. In Sydney, people take very strong approaches to obvious things because they enjoy going in a different direction. And that is why there are often clashes. When I went to Brisbane, the North Americans knocked my socks off with their direct approach. Just play it as it is and develop those moments —it was lovely. But there's a certain point where you look at the way you do it at home, when everyone is comfortable, and realize that it is also an amazing style. The North Americans rely on a lot more focussed skill, I think—very linear, very narrative. The improvisation must follow *a, b, c, d,* and if you jump to *x* or *q* after *p,* then you are really rocking the boat.

I think that, country to country, the seeds get planted in different places. It's the same plant, but they really start to grow differently—different sizes, or they grow bushier or straighter or weedier, or they lean to the wind in different directions.

MELBOURNE

Chrissy Best

In Melbourne, well, in Australia, theatresports is really big. We have a big audience. We perform in the main theatre complex in town. So we have audiences of around eight hundred a Sunday night. And we have a grand finale—we've had two a year for the last couple of years, which have played to two thousand people. The last one was to twenty-seven hundred in the big space in Melbourne. The concert hall. Personally I don't like that so much 'cause it's like doing acting with semaphore flags.

When it first started in Melbourne, it was related to a theatre company called the Playbox Theatre Co. They were the people who administered theatresports. There was no artistic direction. We [the players] got no feedback. We just came in and played and left. And I organized a meeting of players and got them together and said, "Well, this is stupid. We are the players, we run it, we have ideas. No one from this theatre company even comes and sees the show, and they take all the money from it." It was a fairly big money spinner. "We should form our own theatre company and control it ourselves." So we had a meeting of players, and they decided, yes. And it took about three months—we were doing the copyright through Sydney— and we did it then through Canada. And we sent up submissions to Sydney saying, you know, we had formed an actor's company, and we wanted to administer theatresports ourselves. We had various negotiations with them, and we got rights to do it. So we formed the Flying Pig Company. We run theatresports and have the license for Melbourne.

Personally my feeling in the way we do it in Melbourne is that it's very competitive. It's very gaggy. And even at intervals, the teams don't talk together. There is this real separation. We don't do a warm-up, we don't do—we never have notes; we don't have feedback. So I have slated another night in Melbourne, Monday nights, called Pigment of the Imagination, like the Flying Pigs. Basically the Flying Pig meant that if we can run our theatre company then pigs can fly. Sort of that philosophy.

CANBERRA

David Callen

I studied drama for seven years at school. I wanted to be regarded as a serious young actor. The primary reason I was attracted to theatresports was that I'd seen it on TV. So I went and saw a night of it. I thought it was the most amazing fun I'd ever had.

After playing theatresports, I found the humour, the comedy in even the most serious and depressing of speeches. I think it has freed me up. I have a video of this play I did before I started playing theatresports and then another show about six months after I started playing. The first show I was very stiff, very rigid, very serious. The second show I seemed to be a lot more natural, a lot more relaxed, a lot more at ease. I think it's a wonderful training.

[The nature of Aussie rules . . .] Canberra theatresports is very young. The average age for it would be eighteen to twenty-three. I'm an old player and I'm twenty-three. I have a guy on a team who is about twenty-seven, twenty-eight, and he's a bit old to be playing theatresports. It's treated a bit like it's something for kids. It's a young game, energetic and very exuberant and not always very well directed. But it's growing and that's the main thing.

If you look at the sports connection, it is very gladiatorial—only the cast is not thrown to the lions at the end of the show. Four people going up against the world. The audience is there pulling for you. Every time someone gets up there, they want to see you succeed.

We had a problem for a while with one team. They only saw the "sport" in theatresports. They didn't see "theatre." So whenever they got a mark they didn't like, they wouldn't leave the stage. They would stand there and argue with the judges, which really put a damper on the evening. Now in sports, someone arguing with the umpire is all part of the fun, but in theatresports that is not part of the game. It's not pretty and it shouldn't go on.

PERTH

Michael Sanderson-Green

We were both at an acting school.

Angela Sanderson-Green

I left when Michael left, and we just did nothing for a couple of years and just thought, well, maybe that was a part of our life—that we did some theatre and now we don't. Then theatresports arrived in Perth.

Michael Sanderson-Green

Somebody on the beach said he heard of this thing where you go to the theatre and you are given titles and you play games and that they were looking for teams. We said, "Okay, and we know somebody else who might be interested so we'll come along to the first workshop." An actress from Sydney who'd played theatresports there approached a theatre company and asked if she could put it on and run a couple of workshops.

Angela Sanderson-Green

She ran only two workshops, which basically taught the theatresports game format and nothing about the concept of improvisation. Basically "Poem is four of you get up and rhyme," sort of thing. And theatresports ran like that for one and a half seasons. Then suddenly it closed down because the director of the theatre didn't like it. We arrived on Sunday night to play, and there was a sign on the door saying it no longer existed.

Michael Sanderson-Green

Our initial attraction to it wasn't necessarily the theatre of it. We took it as an intellectual exercise. That's how it was originally presented to us. This is how you can beat these games. Some people couldn't do it without drinking. How could you make yourself safe on stage and what format could you use that the audience wouldn't pick up that we could safely do every time. So for the first year that's what we did. We spent hours analysing each game to make them safe. Not improvising them at all . . . well, we did improvise to a certain extent.

Angela Sanderson-Green

For Murder Endowments, we had a system worked out so that in the first few seconds of someone coming on, they knew exactly what was going to happen, and then you played out the same four minutes. In those days, we also had thirty seconds to talk about things before we actually did them. You could actually almost script it. We didn't even call it improvisation. I guess we didn't have a term for it; it was something fun to do. The audience was good. There were lots of them, and they were very enthusiastic. The judging was atrocious.

Michael Sanderson-Green

It was a chance for us to work in a theatre environment. We

enjoyed the workshop way of working. We'd meet every week, two or three times, and run through things. It was noncommittal, and we didn't have to learn the script.

Angela Sanderson-Green

I don't think any of us particularly liked learning scripts and doing the same play night after night.

Michael Sanderson-Green

It's always new, it's always different, it's always learning something. I've found that straight theatre doesn't always offer me that. You tend to keep going over the same things. Improvisation seems to have an extra dimension to it. There is a learning process while you are doing a scripted show, whereas theatresports is that major discovery all the time. On Sunday afternoons, even when I'm not playing, I get a little bit taller.

Angela Sanderson-Green

Straight theatre doesn't give that same buzz. I can remember doing scripted stuff where I would actually fall asleep before going onstage, which doesn't happen anymore in improvisation. There's that lovely feeling like you just don't know what's going to happen each evening once you step on the stage. Also, the people. People are not fearful, and that makes them much more interesting than actors in a straight theatre system.

Michael Sanderson-Green

In Perth, there's a strong competitive element. The audience seems to demand that. You can't just say, "Yeah, we'll make a competition that isn't really a competition." Because when we have a short season with no objective, no grand finale, the audiences don't come. So we have an eleven-week season that culminates in semifinals and grand finals. We do scratch matches occasionally, for our own benefit, but the audience likes to identify with teams. When theatresports first started, we fostered that. We had buttons and people in the audience with streamers, shouting and chanting and all that sort of thing. We play in an old aircraft hanger that's been converted into a music club. You can seat about four hundred on the grand finals. We average about two hundred.

Angela Sanderson-Green

We constantly try to change and look at new formats. Certainly after our experience at the EXPO in Brisbane, we changed the very strictness of the way we play, and it became a lot more open. With more open challenges, it felt a lot more comfortable. We are in the process of developing further. Although the audience is demanding a certain competition, we also feel that the players need to look at how we keep ourselves interested and extended. I suppose we suffer a lot from the "tall poppy syndrome," which is very much an Australian syndrome. Whoever's on top, you cut them off. We see that right through the Australian lifestyle. We like nothing better than to see our top team beaten.

Michael Sanderson-Green

We're running into a bit of bureaucracy under the Belvoir Street Theatre in Sydney. We want to branch out from that system and go directly to Loose Moose. We are too far away from Sydney.

[We've received news that this last bit of information has changed. Angela and Michael indicate that their group now

works directly under Loose Moose and has recently formed
Friends of Theatresports, which will run the season.]

HOBART

Nigel Curtain Smith

I currently produce theatresports in Hobart. Being a production manager has its very stressful side. Making sets and
planning drives you absolutely nuts. What attracted me to theatresports was there seemed to be absolutely nothing to do
beforehand. How wrong I was!

Theatresports was initially suggested by a fellow named
Martin Brown who had heard from his friend who had seen the
first show of theatresports in Sydney about five years ago [1985].
We are the organization that first put on theatresports in
Hobart at the Performing Arts Club. It's a small one-hundred-
seat performing venue behind the Theatre Royal. The Theatre
Royal is the oldest theatre in Australia.

There was a crisis at the Performing Arts Club. The phone
bill had to be paid, and there was a huge cash flow problem. We
were in dire straits. A benefit had to be organized hastily. Everyone was fairly exhausted and not much interested in rehearsing
anything. And Martin suggested this thing he had heard about
called theatresports. The only information he had was that
there were set time limits on games. One was called Poem,
another called Word at a Time, another was Opera. We made up
a whole list of other games, and we set up a chocolate wheel.
Teams ranged from anything from two people to fifteen people.
The evenings bordered on being complete disasters, and the
worst thing we had ever done. But we were hooked! Well, we
solved the initial urgent cash problem. We called it "Off the
Cuff: A Night of Theatresports." This was prior to any contact
with Belvoir Street or any other centre at all. The money went to
helping this company of cooperative theatre workers like
myself and some other people about the town. Theatresports
helped put this company in a position to set themselves up to

apply for grants. And now, five years later, it's the State Theatre Company of Tasmania. It's had all these direct benefits, a fabulous catalyst.

To understand how we play is to understand the nature of Tasmania itself. It's a bizarre cul-de-sac of the Commonwealth. It's an island with unique animals and a unique way of going about things. No one would ever go there if they didn't have to. It's a staggering statistic that every person under the age of twenty-four leaves Tasmania for at least one year, and three quarters of those never come back. But they do; they visit. So staggered throughout the year we have people coming home all the time. They need to be able to walk into a game if they like, without any prep or whatever. So the situation and the style of play we have over here is an impromptu one. So that a person, like a rock and roll star, could walk in and have a good time on stage. Theatresports is a fairly genuine community.

At the end of that first season, we said, "Let's get our shit together." We wrote to Belvoir and asked about a license. They sent us this little rule book and told us to send them five percent and da de da, and we have the franchise so don't you do anything naughty. We refer to that method of theatresports [described in the rule book] as the Colour By Number version. You can use that book if you like. Now don't get me wrong. Lyn Pierce, bless her, planted the seed, the Colour By Numbers seed of theatresports in all the capital cities and Hobart was one. We followed that fairly religiously for the first two years, and then it became very frustrating. People were attempting to "break the rules" and getting penalized by getting poor points. We started to think this was fairly dead-end, this impro business.

Then we went to the Australian National Tournament, and we did really badly. But I was selected to go on a scratch team with a rep from Perth, one from Brisbane, one from Victoria, to form a team to go to the Brisbane EXPO. There I met all these goofy, wacky people from Calgary, New York and from all over. And I thought, A-ha! As soon as I get home I'm going to get that Colour by Numbers and chuck it out the window! When I got home we tried a variety of things, and we had a season in '88 that was all over the place. We tried everything. We tried a mixture and from that we evolved what we like to regard as a truly international playing style, or at least that's what we tell the local media.

We have three judges and a ref. In that role, I'm a complete fascist for the evening. I direct the evening, I side coach and do all the things that need to be done. But the judging, the statistics, all the hype is bullshit, simply that. It's based on World Championship Wrestling. So there's lots of booing the judges and that sort of stuff. We deliberately rig the evening. If a team gets twenty points ahead we'll have a big upset. We'd sacrifice a team to risk all the points in a One-on-One—stuff like that. We get outrageous letters saying the judges should be hung and burnt. I love that hype. We promote it heavily, the hype, the blood, the action! Just between you and me, it's not actually real. It's like wrestling. We tried to get rid of the competition and the audience didn't like it, so we brought it back in a bizarre sort of way. We are very comfortable with our structure now.

It has actually spoiled me in a great way. All this improvising. I resent being a slave to some author, somewhere in some other place. Let's face it, most of the authors in history haven't come from Australia or Tasmania. What I like about impro is it is very immediate. It can deal with concerns that concern us right now.

I'm the only child I know who escaped his entire education without having to play on a single team. Never did sports. I wasn't sickly. I was into music, played trumpet, sang in the choir. Theatresports is the most I've ever had to do with sports in my entire life. I never thought I'd do it at all. I'm glad we found this hype option because it's a great relief to me. If it had come down to real competition, I think I would have had to give it up.

I would like to become a better storyteller. I'm more interested in using impro as a teaching aid than in actually being a star myself. I work a lot with youth, young and wild. I think impro is very liberating and very fresh. I think there's a lot to be said for getting this stuff to the youth.

We don't pay anyone in Tasmania. It's a privilege to play. I think what has happened in Melbourne and places like that is they have wrung their own necks in a way. They have cut off their supply. As soon as you close your company and stop the flow of people who have never played before, you are cutting off your own nose.

In Hobart, on any one night, there will be someone on the stage who has never improvised before and perhaps has never been on stage in their entire life. I think it adds an edge. In Hobart, we like bad teams as well. They may not last the whole night, but if someone wants to come from the northeast coast of Tasmania with a team of four all dressed up in their funny hats and have never been to a workshop in their lives, they can. They can walk in and do a couple of skitty things, maybe something they've rehearsed that could be really hideous, you know, make your flesh creep. They'll probably get gonged off. It's an important part of the night. People pay money to see that. We have a saying in Hobart that goes, "When improvisation is good, it is really excellent to see. And when it's bad, it's really, really excellent to see."

Kate Gaul

I think what we do in Hobart is a little bit different. We are much more irreverent and eclectic. We tend to go to the really bizarre combinations of relationships all the time. We don't treat the sponsors like they do here [New Zealand]. We certainly don't treat them badly, but we don't paint their slogans on our backs either. I suppose they are treated in the same gladiatorial way that the team players are treated.

Sue Westwood

I work backstage. I'm a technical person, specifically in lighting. I come from a theatre company where two people do everything in terms of production. I've been playing theatresports for about five years. The lure for me is, and it might sound weird, but the fact that there is no pressure. There is no pressure to come up with the goods. I love that feeling. I don't mind playing a bad game because I still feel every time I come off stage—I feel good that I've been on. I've been there, trying, doing it. I love the spontaneity of it. I think that you're working on a level that is up tight in the top notch of your head. It's like you're not working completely consciously. Something else is happening. I think you push your mind so much further when you are playing. I think theatresports has potential because it's the newest thing to happen in Hobart theatre. It's new and it can be inspired. That's what I want to see. I don't want to see ordinary plays. I want to see something inspired.

NEW ZEALAND

AUCKLAND

Mark Ferguson

I'm a professional actor and also a theatre teacher. I had been involved in theatresports in Sydney as a player and then as a coach with Lyn Pierce. She had been with theatresports pretty much from the beginning in Sydney, and we'd been playing and coaching there for a good three years. There had been a very brief experience with theatresports in New Zealand. It was just a small experiment brought over by another Australian or maybe a New Zealander who had seen it in Australia. It was very, very primitive, but it whet people's appetite.

They thought there might be something in it, so Lyn was invited over for a whirlwind coaching tour, which took in all the major centres in New Zealand. She tended to target the professional actors, and they responded with gusto. Television New Zealand, through one of their art programs, made a feature program on the first public performance of theatresports and a little bit about the workshop process. I was invited over by the producer of that show to assist him with the program because Lyn couldn't actually be there. So Lyn and I worked on getting the first public performance together, and then I continued to work on the program after that. And I stayed.

I remember the first night I ever played. I had never done impro in a performance situation. We don't really have a history of that. Performance impro in Australia and New Zealand tends to be very fringe and unskilled, and professionals tend to pretty much avoid it. But theatresports was a lot more fun. We got honked off in our first game. I remember thinking it was the most terrifying experience I had had in my life. It was real adrenaline.

In New Zealand, we are aiming for a style that promotes improving the standard of play. The highly competitive, highly structured form used in Sydney was terrific for the audiences up to a point. The audiences really like the razzy taz sort of game show aspect of it. But I felt it was giving it the same style of play all the time with the format of the one-, two-, three- and four-minute games. Teams in no way were being encouraged to take risks. You couldn't. You were being timed. And if you wanted to win, you had to play what you were best at. That was very frustrating. I was witnessing some really fabulous performers going absolutely nowhere and getting really bored and frustrated. We had a high turnover of people, and we lost a lot of good people.

Now what we're trying to do in New Zealand is open up our communication, particularly with North American theatresports because it's been going a lot longer there. We've got to keep changing because that seems to be the very nature of it. We are also highly commercial. That's the way it was established here—as a professional actor's cooperative. The trick for us is we have to mix interesting and developing play, getting people into the audience and having them come back. So theatresports is for professional actors, and if you want to play in a professional show you have to join Equity. It also means we have to pay you, which is great. It's what we want to do.

The format that we are playing here at the International Challenge [1990] is not far away from our standard format. We look for things that can be structured and safe for the night and that will be entertaining. We are looking at setting up a couple of other venues during the week so that we could have about three shows running and perhaps start some structured corporate shows. If we can offer people work, we can build a core around that.

To get up and running would be great for us. Theatresports is the purest form of performer's theatre that I have been involved with. When I was in Sydney, I found it really unfortunate that the theatre was becoming design theatre. The designs were taking over, and the performers were getting lost. Designers were directing, and it was becoming madness, whereas doing this, we are trying to develop our shows. Rather than the format controlling the show, it's the performers taking over the show more and more. I think the stage that we are at now is that people are starting to get more courage.

Jay Laga'aia

I'm from the Island of Western Samoa, and I reside here in good old Auckland, New Zealand. I'm a musician first and foremost. I don't come from a dramatic background. I come out of South Auckland where drama is pretending you're sick and not going to school. That's as far as it goes. I think that's the beauty of theatresports, that you don't need the dramatic background; you just need to be hungry, I suppose.

I was introduced to theatresports about four years ago when it was first introduced to New Zealand. As a musician, a singer working the floors, you learn to ad lib and learn to use your audience. I've always been quick off the mark when it came to using what I could see and what I'd heard, compiling it into something and feeding it back to the audience. People appreciate that. That's why I got interested in the concept of theatresports and have been playing it ever since.

When you talk about "theatre" to a Polynesian, performing is something that just comes naturally because it is part of your lifestyle. Dance is a form of language because language is by word of mouth, by hand action and by song. That's how stories and legends are passed on, so performing is just something that comes natural to you. The object for Polynesians and Indigenous People of this country is to get a proper job. So when you talk about theatre they say, "That's fine, but you know, what do you do for a living?"

I'm the only person from my community that has claimed theatresports that I know of. I play regularly. I enjoy it and I encourage a lot of my relations and a lot of the brown race to get into it. Especially with my young people. I do workshops, and it becomes very acceptable with the parents if you can relate things to the bible. That's the whole trust thing, like in the bible, "Ask and it shall be given; seek and you shall find." And you know, Polynesians—they're a work of art. They're just dying of laughter. They will laugh at anything. It is always a sense of community. Always a sense of humour, because what else is there? If you can't laugh, what else is there?

The attraction for me is the fellowship. I like meeting not only the top actors, but people in general. Also the creation. I've found that theatresports itself is a natural buzz. You have your "off" days and your "on" days, but it's never the same. Being "on" means gaining the rhythm of the group. When that happens, you can taste it tomorrow. You are creating things that just go. If it flies, it flies. It has also taught me to accept dying on stage—say, "Oh well," and laugh it off and go on. The worst thing is winning and knowing you shouldn't have.

Since theatresports has happened, for me, it's added a couple of inches. Inches not only to my stature but to my own kind of knowledge. I want to stress that theatresports is something that everybody can play. Meeting all these people with different accents and finding out that everybody has a unified accent on stage.

WELLINGTON

Liz Melaine

What happened was Lyn [Pierce] from Australia came over, and she did workshops for actors. Downstage Theatre, which is a main theatre in Wellington, started playing. But it was really, really raw stuff. We played the old way where you toss, and the winner of the toss chooses the game. You both have to play the same game. That was all we knew, so that was fine. But then the Brisbane EXPO came up, and we had a national final. Out of the national final . . . we sent the winning team, which was the Auckland team. Plus one person from each of the centres to make up a team, which was awful, really, because we had just started playing. And to then end up playing with people we didn't even know and had never met until we got there was a bit of a nightmare.

Plus the whole format was entirely different. It was like we were the local football team—*suddenly* finding out they were playing at the world cup, and it was unbelievable. I remember just sitting there with my mouth open at the kind of stuff that was going on. Watching the Calgary team, Tony [Totino] and Dennis [Cahill]. When we came back, I thought, This is fantastic! The way they are playing is exciting, and there is a lot of risk and challenge. I couldn't understand where the way we'd been playing it had come from. So Annie and I said to all the players who were waiting for us to come back with new games and things, we just said, "Forget the way we've been playing because we are not playing like that ever again."

HOLLAND

Kathy Destephino

I am here from Rotterdam, Holland, and maybe it is helpful to say immediately that I am an American who is living and working in Holland, so I've moved there. That is my home now.

I first saw theatresports at a performance in New York City about five or six years ago. I saw a performance and I bought this book [*Impro: Improvisation and the Theatre*, Keith Johnstone, 1979]. I invited my friends over and we tried to figure out what it was. Then about six months later, Keith came and taught in 1987, a long weekend in Holland. So that group was made up of fifty percent actors and fifty percent teachers. After that spring workshop in '87, a lot of the people who took part in it went home and tried to get it together. So the first actual theatresports performance was in December–January '88.

At that time, there were four different groups in Holland. There was one in Amsterdam, one in Utrecht and two groups in Rotterdam. We performed with each other, and once every three weeks there was a gig. Small houses. We weren't very good, and then somewhere in the middle of that first season, a group of Dutch people went over to London and met Theatresports London. A couple of the people who teach there know Keith very well and did things in Theatre Machine. So we had a lot of traffic between London and Holland in that beginning six months.

The reactions of our audiences so far have been very positive. It amazes me how positive the action continues to be. You know, if they saw a proper theatresports match, it would just blow them away because they've seen us first, you know, struggling.

ENGLAND

Melanie Miller

Theatresports arrived in London with Barry Cook [Loose Moose production manager in the mid-eighties]. He stuck a note on the common notice board asking if there was anyone in London interested in playing theatresports, as I remember it. It was in the fall of 1987. I think that I did perform, and I managed to fall off the stage.

When theatresports first started, probably fifty percent of the people involved were not English. They were New Zealanders, Americans, Australians, Canadians or Brits who had travelled a lot. It was long after Keith had left [England], and there was no improvisation or very, very little. Most of it was taught badly. Theatre Machine carried on for a while, but it's dormant now. The people involved teach—they teach a lot of mask stuff, but they rarely teach out of London.

Barry Cook

When I left Loose Moose, Keith kind of gave his blessing to go forth and propagate. At first, I went to Vancouver and with some of the original Vancouver players, started an Alternative Theatresports. Then I found myself in Edmonton where I worked with Theatre Network's theatresports. I decided to go to London in '86. There's a place there called the Actor's Centre. They have a huge call-board. I just posted a note, "Does anyone know theatresports?" Alan Marriott replied. He'd been with Vancouver and had gone to England to study at LAMDA, I believe. He was working with people who were preparing an impro Hamlet, most of whom were Australians and Americans and called themselves, "Marginal Bard." We got together several times and discussed what we thought it should look like and decided that, as a "sporting event," it should reflect British soccer—"football"—complete with referees and yellow and red card offences.

We put together a version at the Cricklewood Production Village under the auspices of Marginal Bard. Audiences were tiny as Cricklewood was an awful place to find. We'd started a series of workshops, and about that time a fellow named Andy Harman, an American, showed up. He'd been in contact with Dennis Cahill, and he'd been directed to get in touch with us. He brought some other ideas with him and some people he'd been working with—our first real English performers—people like Lee Simpson and Justin Case.

We got out of Cricklewood and went down to a pub in Balham in South London. A lot of pubs have a function room that's just left empty. That's when we started getting much larger crowds, every Sunday night. We were attracting more performers too still mostly Australians and Americans, and a core group was forming. When we did start to get a lot of British performers in, they were mostly cabaret performers. British "actors" seemed afraid to take the chance of participating in improvisation.

Nica Burns was the artistic director at the Donmar Warehouse, an alternative theatre venue in the West End. She'd contacted us about moving into the Donmar because she had seen theatresports in Australia and liked it, so we transferred over there. I'm trying to remember . . . our one-year contract with Loose Moose was running out, and Nica wanted to take it and put it under her auspices. We had a couple of Theatre Machine people teaching workshops at that time—Desmond Jones and John Muirhead. During this period, the group performed at the Calgary Olympics, the Edinburgh Festival and the Liverpool Comedy Festival.

Now Nica's vision of theatresports was a more instantaneous-get-up-and-perform sort of thing. It was cabaret. We wanted to encourage newcomers, and she wanted stars to perform—and that the Donmar, not the performers, have artistic control.

Around that time, Alan, myself, Melanie, Doug and Tracy had expressed the possibility of: Nica wants theatresports at the Donmar, so we'll go Theatresports London, with the possibility of moving out into the "provinces." I approached Loose Moose with this proposal. The end result is that Keith came across with his lawyer on his way to Scandinavia to do some work-shops. He was going to decide who was going to get the rights. He met with us and led a workshop and a general "Let's talk" session. Finally he said he preferred that it remain in the con-trol of the player's group and those who had worked to build it. So the Donmar said they would have nothing to do with us.

So as a co-op we played the Boulevard Theatre in Soho, the Red Rose in Finsbury and other venues. My problem was that I was out of town a lot doing "legit" tours. I'd come back and teach the occasional workshop or play the evil "hell judge" at a match. I left England in the fall of '91. Theatresports was a sort of mixed bag then. Many of the players were moving on to other impro shows, and there were a lot of up-and-coming per-formers moving in. At the time, coincidentally perhaps, there was a surge of impro-type theatre [and TV—*Who's Line Is It Anyway?*], which helped to build an audience.

Doug Nunn

I'm presently the artistic director of Theatresports UK. I was trained in San Francisco with Barbara Scott and a number of other people. The first match I ever saw was in March 1987, and I signed up for a course that night. There was a real buzz in the air, the same feeling you get as a sports fan, and I'm a real sports kind of guy. The more sporty theatresports is—people yelling foul and stuff—the more I like it. One of the reasons it took me so long to get into theatre was because I was such a sports-aholic. I was like, "Theatre shmeatre. I want to go to the ball game."

So when I saw this theatresports thing, I was like, "God, this is the way it should be done!" I have always thought that particular kind of buzz was really special, and I have really been impressed. It's like you can look at your fellow players and wink at each other and know that you're *on* that night—like when you step up to the plate at the bottom of the ninth and you smack it over the fence or something. It's the same kind of feeling. When it is really working, that's how good you feel. Whatever it is, it has been there during the funniest times that I have improvised.

My partner and I came over here [to London] and started working on a stand-up double comedy act just on a lark. We started meeting other people who were doing improvisation here. There was a fairly large group of people interested in theatresports at that time, but they were sort of off it at the time. Until August '87 in Edinburgh, we did a one off thing at the Festival with those same people from London.

This was another one of those buzzes. We went into this huge hall with four hundred drunks. At midnight. The crowd was really drunk, and they have a reputation for really hammering people. Here in Britain, it's really hard to stay on stage some nights. People were not in a good mood. And we went up there and said, "Theatresports!" and within three minutes, they were in the grip of our hand. We did a half-hour demo match. They loved it, they went wild, they encored and everything. I was completely shocked. I didn't expect they would like us at all. Had it been a cabaret situation, they would have booed us off the stage.

When we came back to London in the fall of '87, we sort of co-enlisted about fifteen to twenty people who were fairly interested. Workshops led to the beginning of theatresports being staged. We had twice-a-week workshops for a month leading up to the first match. November of '87 at the Donmar Warehouse. It's a West End venue that holds a fairly large crowd. When Tracy and I left in August of '88, it seemed to have a very promising future. When we got back in November '89, it was a disgruntled group of people. Different people have different notions about what they want to see come out of theatresports. We had numerous political disputes. I'm sure you are aware of the kind of stuff that goes on. We broke off in the spring of '88 and set out what was to become Theatresports UK. Keith came over to mediate the situation.

Melanie Miller

We just had a big tournament, which was very successful. It was our first tournament in the UK. Theatresports has started to catch within the theatrical community here. We have trained probably four to five hundred people. We have a fairly solid workshop group and six-week courses that run back to back throughout the year. Through the workshops a lot of people have come to play theatresports or to set up their own group.

We have about half a dozen teachers who are of a high standard. People from the Theatre Machine, people who have worked with Lecoque in Paris. Now our teachers teach specific areas of improvisation. There's a generation of players who have taught in drama schools and other schools as well. They teach foundation courses, and the courses, which, thanks to Doug and Tracy, are very carefully laid out. They put a lot of stuff down on paper; they're very good at getting stuff down on paper. Quite often we have jamming sessions. People just get together without a teacher and have a workshop.

Doug Nunn

For the last six months, we've spent a lot of time digging

ourselves out of real problems. But very little artistically has been done because we've been busy with all the pragmatic kinds of things. The matches here right now have been exciting on and off, but no one is venturing into new territory. Now we have written a new constitution for the group, starting up next month, which will be player-based. What I hope is going to happen is a player-based group that runs its own affairs efficiently and does a good job of it.

NORWAY

Kyrre Hangen Bakke

I was in a play, and at the first read through they said, "We'll do some improvisation," and I froze! "I am too old for this, I don't want to do it, I'm hopeless at improvisation." I used to hate it in drama school. I would feel that I had to take responsibility for everything. And I would always feel that I ought to be champion of the world. I like to play games, but it never occurred to me that playing games could be a good way of learning about acting.

Anyway, this director knew about theatresports. I think he had been to classes with Keith. So he started every rehearsal for five weeks with improvisational games. Gradually he taught us a bit about it, and he was rather good. After about four weeks, we attended a three-day course with Keith Johnstone in Oslo. This was in the spring of 1985 I think. So that was my first encounter with the technique.

Later that year, we had been having some workshops in the autumn, and just before Christmas, we did two public shows. The first one was a huge success, beginner's luck. The feeling was amazing. The improvisors were so amazed at what they could do even though the storytelling might not have been so good. The second show wasn't quite so good. Couldn't be, right? That time the audience was drama students who wanted to be funnier than the ones on stage. They would rather see something destruct than see something work. After those two shows, nothing much happened for eighteen months or so. Then we started to pick it up again, and we have been doing it sporadically for five years. And now it's growing. Keith has been a number of times to Norway. I think he has done two acting courses, one for teachers and one for dramatists. We've been doing regular shows once a month in Oslo.

It has been, up till now, exclusively professional actors on the stage. The rookie situation is kind of unresolved. We fell into this trap. The rookies are training but not playing. The players are playing but not training. Which is absurd really. I've been unhappy about this for more than two years. The general things that we're up against are the usual things. Jokes, gagging, people turning on personal charm. We had a meeting and decided to tighten things up—notes after the show, things like that, that we haven't been doing. Because people don't get paid, this tends to mean people will come in for the show and then leave the show going, "Hoo, hoo, we are great!" So we want to start training seriously. If you are not training, you are not in the show. We'll also start doing ten-minute warm-up games with the rookies and get them into circulation.

We have not been very good at dividing up the evenings. We usually have a mixture of the Danish game or a Revised Challenge or a game with judges. This is something we learned from the Danes. We use red and green cardboard. One team is the red team, the other the green team, so people can root for their teams by voting. I think it's a good thing at the Moose that the audience is screaming instead. People can let it out and things are decided faster. Sometimes it will take forever to count the vote. And we have tried the compere. I did it once and I thought I could learn, but I stopped doing it after four shows because I would much rather be on stage with the others. We haven't had any Free Impro like the Allstar Show yet, but we did steal something from the Danes called the Impro Café.

Also, a habit we picked up from the Danes was the habit of selling to any audience member two roses and one wet sponge that they can throw on stage when they feel like it. The Danish audiences are so well behaved and objective. It worked for a while in Oslo and then people started bringing their own wet sponges, very wet. Then it became an outlet for people who just wanted to see something go wrong. So we're probably going to stop that and let them scream and boo and hiss instead. Another thing which is different is the honking. I think the Swedes do it by letting the judges hold up a zero sign. I do tend to agree with Keith that if you zero or honk a scene you probably shouldn't give it a score of one.

We have been learning so many new things here [at the International Impro School in Calgary]. I can't wait to get back and teach the Hat Game. We've been doing stupid mistakes that anybody would be doing for the first year or two. It will be fun to delve into that game and see how far you can go before you take the hat. Yeah!

Helen Vikstvedt

I sort of found my way with improvisation. It suits me because traditionally in the theatre we take three steps to the left and turn, and then we speak. I mean the old way of directing the old plays. I don't like that very much. I think it is quite boring. Improvisation is helping me with my acting.

I have been doing theatresports professionally for one year. The Theatresports Union in Norway has more than fifty members. Theatresports attracts very young people, and Oslo has about fifteen actors. It is a sort of status thing because most Norwegian actors are in the age of thirty, thirty-five, forty. And they are sort of afraid of going up there and making a fool of themselves. They are well-known actors with a status, and they can't bear it. Maybe they come once, and then you don't see them again.

I think what we are doing is going for the laughter—making funny characters and it is never truthful. That's one of the things I want to learn. I'm impressed with the way that the Canadians can improvise and do it very seriously. I see good actors who still go very far with characters. We have to have more training. Once a month is not often enough, and then you have to practice in front of an audience to know what you need to work on.

GERMANY

Jochen Baum

In Tubingen we started in September 1989.

Conny Fruhauf

The artistic director, Volker Quandt, came from Denmark. He's a German, but he lived in Denmark for ten years and also in Sweden. When he came to Tubingen he told us from the beginning that he would like to do theatresports. But we had never heard of it before. We are the first group to do theatresports in Germany.

Jochen Baum

For me, it was to be spontaneous, to be really alone and find something that is going on in your mind, like a mountain to climb on. Very interesting and a challenge.

Conny Fruhauf

I think it is very good training to develop a group playing together, to listen to each other, play together, to really know each other. This technique has helped us a lot to find a common language when we are rehearsing for other plays. So you can say, "play Low Status or High Status," and everybody knows what it is.

We have seen what they do in Sweden, and for us it is quite different. What we do is from the Danish model. . . . Every suggestion comes from the audience, and they judge after every scene. We only have one judge in the second half. We have a live musician off stage, and we have also what Vanessa does with cassettes. We only knew the Danish model and did not know that there were other ways to do it. What we learned in this workshop [at the International Impro School] is very good. I don't think you have to have every suggestion come from the audience because it blocks you in a way as an actor.

Jochen Baum

Here [in Canada] the actors are more relaxed and not always so competitive.

Conny Fruhauf

I think the contact between the audience and the actors is more direct. Friends who have seen theatresports for the first time have said that it is what the audience wants to see. They want to see how you do theatre, what theatre is in its pure character. They like that you can take part, react and be much more a part of the atmosphere.

Jochen Baum

On the other hand, they like to watch the technique, like in soccer sometimes.

Conny Fruhauf

We are a theatre for children and young people, so we have that kind of audience. They come back again and again, and that's good because they normally don't go to theatre at all. In Germany, there are some people working in theatre that know the book *Impro [Impro: Improvisation and the Theatre*, Keith Johnstone, 1979] and something about the technique, but they don't know theatresports at all. Some say, "Oh, it is very good, amazing and spontaneous," and others say, "It's not my idea of theatre. It's superficial. You can't go into scenes. It is too short."

They say it is not an art. So maybe Germans have another idea of theatre. But there are more and more people getting interested in theatresports.

Jochen Baum

They say it's just an entertainment come from America, uh sorry, Canada. There's a generation break in theatre in Germany. There's a need for a theatre for young audiences and a theatre for old people. I'm from a generation with TV, and theatresports has some ideas, some techniques like TV with music and fast scenes.

She Said, He Said

WOMEN IN THEATRESPORTS

Men have always outnumbered women on the stage at the Loose Moose Theatre. From the beginning, the lack of women's involvement in theatresports was discussed, and although many women attended classes and had their debut on stage, few remained to play theatresports over a long period. Kathleen Foreman remembers that the Moosettes, the first opposing theatresports team, described themselves as "three slightly balding guys and a chick"—indicative not just of the male-to-female ratio but of the roles women often have to play. One particular memory of Kathleen's seems to capture the experience of many women theatresports players.

"The scene is drawing to a close. Suddenly I'm picked off my feet and tucked under the arm of one of my teammates. He bellows, 'I've got the girl, you grab the beer and let's go!' As the ultimate prop, I'm carried off stage and put down amongst the hats and coats."

Veena Sood

I am still single because I play theatresports, and it's commonly known that as women in theatresports, you will remain single. 'Cuz funny girls aren't as attractive as funny guys. That's the problem.

Rick Hilton

My name is Rick Hilton, I am married to a wonderful woman

and I have a little baby girl, so that's what happens to male improvisors.

Veena Sood

They have a personal life.

Carol Hazenfield

I often feel that theatresports here in San Francisco has a very feminine kind of energy to it. Meaning that we, I feel, listen better—we're on a different pacing a lot of times. . . . The improvisors here leave each other space. If you don't talk for five seconds someone isn't going to charge in and start yammering or push you physically aside, and people don't leap on stage making huge physical offers, which I find intimidating as a player and as a woman. If I feel I'm being sort of manhandled emotionally or with a physical dynamic, I'll shrink up. I don't think we do a lot of that here.

They've done language studies—and this is in a lot of different places in the western world anyway—men interrupt each other and women . . . some huge, astronomical amount more than women interrupt men. And in theatresports where you're kind of always interrupting and making offers if your social tendency is to wait until someone is totally done, if there's a man in the scene or ready to come into the scene, then *boom* they'll be there ahead of you. I know that here I'll feel railroaded over the top if I'm playing with certain men. Not all of them.

As well, men don't think of themselves in terms of "us." A man doesn't have to have a woman or a woman's approval or stamp of affirmation in order to be important to other men or in order to be successful. But we do. I mean, I think we think we do, and I think society makes us think that way. In improv, where it goes by so quickly, if you're working on a different rhythm—like my stage rhythms are usually pretty slow, and I try and give myself time to be affected by something that happened—you don't have those openings very often. And I've had people say, "Jump out there," you know? Men say, "Get off the bench"—not even "Get off the bench" but "Make your offers faster" or whatever. I don't want to change the way I find my way through a scene. I'm not talking about acting, pacing. I'm talking about the way I assimilate information, process it and spit it back out. And I don't think men want to wait.

Cathleen Rootsart

I'm also in a league where there are practically no women. For a while there, I was pretty much the only woman. When I was in New York, I went to this tournament where they invited a team from each city for a couple of weeks. It was in '86 or '87. All the years run together! Their league was almost totally women, and they were really amazed by our league, which was almost totally men. I think it depends on how the league starts. Once it becomes a jocular male thing, you know, it's really hard for women to break in. Maybe it's sort of a question of needing to be able to wrestle with the boys. It's like that in so many things. It's like—Was Margaret Thatcher really a woman or was she just a man with breasts? Do you know what I mean?

I think that the female stereotypes come to the surface easily. So that if you're in a scene and you're improvising with someone and all of a sudden it becomes this weird sexual thing, or you're the ditsy secretary, it's easy to go back to the stereotype because you're not blocking. I think that everybody knows where the easy laughs are, and if you're dying, sometimes survival instinct kicks in and the audience will reward you for that and will reward the men for that as well. The audience will reward you for that behaviour—dick grabbing and stuff—and won't have the patience to sit through something that's maybe a little moving or intellectually stimulating or truthful in any way, shape or form.

I wrote a scene that talks about a lot of issues of being a woman today and the beauty myth culture and stuff like that. I'm always torn between wanting to write something about just being a person because I don't want to necessarily be the "woman" of the troupe all the time and like "Oh, there's the woman dealing with women's issues," you know? Sometimes it's important and it's rewarding for me. There are a couple of points in the show where I can only hear women laughing and I like that a lot, but I think that the next time that I write something I won't necessarily be dealing with women's issues again. This is my summer to read feminist literature.

Very often, men would rather pick a team of all men and play women, than choose to have a woman on the team. High voices, very meek, never ever strong women, or if they are strong women, they are bitches and old cows who slapped people with their handbags, you know. I've played a man, I think, once.

Clare Serrif

I think that women are still definitely on the make to look good to the opposite sex at all times, whatever that is to them—like hair and makeup or by the way they act or the way they dress. Yeah, I think it's inhibiting.

I find that it's harder to get women to that point of abandon, that sense of abandon in their character or into what they are doing—that sort of abandon that's forgetting about your body and just doing what's necessary. I find it harder to get them out of the sort of posing thing or the fixing-their-hair thing on stage. I find abandon is one of the biggest things for me that will bring a guy out of the workshops into the performance quicker than a girl. That barrier takes longer to break through. I think it's instilled in us—the way you sit, the way you behave—to catch a mate.

Denalda Williams

We were doing workshops, and he [Keith Johnstone] was going on about death and violence, and you know, I said, "Well

Keith," I said, "I don't think we have to be violent, and I don't think we have to die all the time. You know, I think we are clever enough that we could get around this violence and stuff like that." And you know, Keith sort of dismissed me that time. But the next day he went—he couldn't remember my name. He said, "Where is that girl, where's that girl, that girl from Vancouver? Oh . . . Miss Violence?" He said, "You know, you're right." And I had a tremendous amount of respect that he had thought about it. I thought he'd dismissed me, but he was just, I think, mulling. That was something that he mulled over, and he said, "You know, you're right. There is a lot of death and violence in it because we don't have enough women."

Paul Bernardo

First off you get a tremendous amount of guys coming to theatresports at a late teen, early twenties age, who are working out the, um . . . maturity process. Guys, I think, can team up better than women—because guys play team sports, in my day anyway, more than women play team sports. And that's changing. As is everything related to women and equality of work and the recognition to be able to do a job just as good as anybody else. So I think you will see that change.

The second part of my comment is that I think women have an extra hurdle to get over that the males that are drawn here, to theatresports, don't have; and that is, I think it is easier for guys to make fun of themselves and make themselves the butt of a joke than it is for a woman. Because society is saying that she should be pretty and sugar and spice and everything nice and look real, you know, pretty. And so it is difficult for performers to be Lucille Ball. To be a very beautiful woman that can be hysterically funny but in an instant turn back to being very beautiful. Man, that is—that's real hard to do. But I think more and more women will venture out and do it.

And, you see, our audiences are mostly women. If you look at our audience over the long haul, and the months, we draw more women than men. Which I find real interesting because, at best, we are starting to get two females in the classes [improvisation classes], and we've often worked with one. So there's that, there's the other hurdle, that the female has to come to terms with her self-image, the fact that she's a comedian. "Oh, you're *funny?*" What does that mean? Does that mean you are any less feminine? Or any less an attractive woman? I can't answer that because I'm not female. That's just my perspective.

The other thing too . . . I'm going to say things about some of the males that come because they are also working through some stuff. And when the male–female thing comes together (although we have some very talented improvisors around), when they are developing, they can be pretty childish and pretty crass, and when you're a team and you are doing locker-room kind of jarbing amongst the team . . . it is different if you're a female.

I'm sick and tired of listening to guys' stupid dick jokes and innuendoes that are flying around. An awful lot of women get, frankly, really turned off by it. When I was director of workshops, it was one thing I addressed with the women a lot. And it is a very difficult thing to do. I would say, "Okay, do you want me to go up to Bob and say quit being a chauvinist jerk asshole, or how can I say that to him? I think it's better that *you* say that to him."

I brought it in, but I don't think anyone remembers it, but I remember it because I went through absolute shit for it because I got blasted from both sides at first. I, as workshop director, said, "We are going to have an all-female workshop. Directed by a female, Linda Kash." Well, the guys—"What's so special about them? Like, why do they need their own workshop?" And I said, "I don't know, but I think they do." And the first thing I know was, "What the fuck is the matter with you? Why do you think we need our own workshop?" Well, they went to the workshop, and that was great, you know, because a little bit of it was male bashing. You know—"These guys are fucking assholes. You know? They are fucking goddamn stereotypes." I mean, at our meeting after one of the early shows here, you know . . . the only female on the cast said, "Hey, I'm sick and tired of being your *fucking* girlfriend, your *fucking* mother and your *fucking* wife, you know. Give me a break!" This blew up after a show, I mean, she just went, "Did you know that tonight I was a whore *twice*, a housewife, a mother and a nurse." But the problem was that we only have one woman in the cast, and when a scene would go in that direction . . . who has to play the part. Well, right after she said that, we brought wigs in because, you know, she said, "I'm not going up there. Paul, you go be the fucking whore." And we did. And then we did less of it. Because you get in there, and you go through that, and that wasn't fun shit. That was cheap humour.

Rebecca Stockley

There are few women in improvisation, and there are few women in comedy as well. That's one part of it. One theory is that as young women, as young children, we are not given reinforcement for being funny. And boys are, you know, encouraged to be funny and comical, and girls are to be pretty and quiet.

Denalda Williams

I don't know, cause I think *I'm* funny, and I don't know why it is. It is just who I am. I go out there and I do what I do and people laugh. I don't think it is because I'm any different than any other woman. It is something about me, whether I was a woman or a man. I don't know how to answer that. I would say probably because [in comedy] you need a thicker skin, and women tend to be a little bit more sensitive.

You're hanging out there on the edge [in comedy], and it *is* a little bit dangerous. It's, you know, you make yourself look foolish. And where society teaches us to be pretty . . . I can't think of Brooke Shields down on all fours acting like a dog with a thorn in its paw. That image doesn't happen for me—whoofing like a goddamn Doberman pincher. *I* can bark like a dog; these are talents I have. Most women don't possess those. I don't know that there is an answer.

Esther Reiss

Men are not funnier than women. Men are more pliable human beings than women because they don't have so many everyday preoccupations with life. Women have a lot more everyday responsibility, and that takes away this surplus, this extra force you have. To, to play . . . you have to have a lot of . . . extra force. The other reason—I think it is the same old story—is that men are more competitive than women. When the workshops or shows compete, the women tend to go off somewhere else.

Morgan Leigh Russell

I think it's the whole male thing of going out and conquering. I know when I first started out with SAK Theatre, there was this guy who trained me and then we would do shows together and I would literally whisper things to him. Whisper ad-libs to him and then let him say it and get the laugh. It's like I knew I wasn't supposed to be funny. Like boys are the funny ones and girls add the niceness and they make the audience feel comfortable.

Linda Rosenfield

My big comment about theatresports in the league in which I play is that it is very much a boy's game. There's all this male energy, an overwhelming sense of desire to control and drive a scene. There's a real lack of trust in women's choices and a lack of trust in women's talent. So what happens is you get kneed and elbowed out of scenes, you get killed a lot, asked to exit, sent out. You rarely get called into a scene unless they need a bimbo, a counter girl or some minor part where you'll end up leaving. I have learned to survive in my league by playing stereotypical roles—because you get squelched for playing a really strong female role. The heroine gets moved off the stage somehow, and then the hero comes in. So I find myself playing really happy characters, things that are easily accepted like the happy mother figure who always has a smile on her face and other pleasing female characters. But I don't do bimbos; I refuse to do bimbos. I've been out in the business community for ten years, and my experience with theatresports is not much different than my experience in business. It's still a boy's world.

Denalda Williams

You know, it brings around the other question: Why do the guys get laid after the show and not the chicks?

You know, I can remember those days when Tony [Totino] and Dave [Duncan] and all those guys . . . the women would swarm around them. Those were the days, my friend. In Vancouver it is the same thing, you know. The guys get groupies. I get the nice family in from Port Coquitlam. "We think you are so! You are our favourite." And then they want to take you next door to McDonalds. "Can we buy you a shake, honey?"

Funny men are sexy. Funny women are funny.

Rebecca Stockley

Funny women are the plague or castrating ball breakers. Never date a guy that you are funnier than.

Lisa Merchant

It's like, little boys walk faster than little girls. You know, there is no reason for it, but little boys just walk faster than little girl babies. And, you know, I think it takes longer for girls in the rookie league and I think they get discouraged and it is that high dropout factor.

Denalda Williams

I don't think it will ever be found out as one thing, I mean it is such a . . . Second City have been six with a breakup of four and two [four men and two women] forever, and it is the same thing there. For a long time, I think we have to think of it as breaking ground. Sophie Tucker was the first real female comedian of any kind, and then, you know: Tony Fields, Phyllis Diller . . . that's only thirty, forty years ago. Where we are . . . maybe we are moving fast, you know. Maybe things will be different in twenty years.

Lyn Pierse

I didn't know Keith's training would have had this affect on my writing. Now I can look back and see why all the women I originally trained with are writing. We are writing film, poetry, theatre, stand-up comedy, books. The training in improvisation has released the women. Now I think that theatresports has had a very interesting affect on women. It's because it gives you a sense of creative independence, the process. It enables you to be responsible for the first time in your life for your own learning process.

Gary Campbell

Funny women are as attractive as nonfunny women. I don't find anything unattractive about women being funny. I don't think it would be a conscious decision on any man's part [to exclude women from comedy], although I agree it could be true on a subconscious level. Maybe there is something. Like, "Oh, she is a funny woman, not a woman I am interested in [except] to laugh at her." So who knows, who knows?

I do know that as far as good improvisors go right now, I can probably name just as many, almost as many, good female improvisors right here in Toronto as I can good male improvisors. I mean, I'm sure it would split in favour of the men, but it would be closer than at any other time than I can think of. I mean, we are talking small numbers. I don't know that many good improvisors, constantly good, that can go out there time after time and get whatever the particular job is done. But I know lots of women now that can do it. I think it is a bit of an upsurge and a really welcome one.

Can I say one thing though? I think of the good female improvisors that I know, none of them are assholes, whereas some of the good male improvisors that I know . . . a couple of them are. I think we'll just leave it at that.

Ellen Idelsson

Well, without offending anybody, I find that the cities I've played in in Canada do seem a bit more sexist. A bit behind the times in term of equality. I have noticed there are some sexist attitudes on the stage and in life. People just seem to see women as being inferior or sex objects. In LA we strive for equality and, you know, we enforce it. We put people in their place whenever they get out of line. I mean, we have women in our group in Los Angeles who would get on the stage with a sexist man and immediately he's wearing a Teddy, on his knees and barking like a dog. Sometimes you have to go overboard to prove a point. When we play women against men, the women always win because sometimes the men are just so taken with themselves that they are not really playing. The women balance that out. I think it's good that we have Dan and myself running the company. We support each other, and I feel that we speak strongly for our sexes as, well, sort of role models, I guess.

Tony Totino

It seems that there are equal numbers of women and men who *start* theatresports, who join up for beginners' classes, people who express an interest in getting involved in theatresports. The numbers are equal. In fact, here in Norway, the numbers may even be tilted slightly toward females. I think that might be true in other places as well. But there's something about the process, that tends to, you know, weed the women out of the groups, and I'm talking after a few years, maybe two years perhaps. Maybe there's some element in the work which women find is a problem because, of course, the competitive atmosphere perhaps drives women away, but of course the competitive atmosphere also drives many men away too.

I still think it is perhaps a social phenomenon in that women are even today . . . it's not particularly "correct" for women to sit around a party or something like that and crack hilariously funny jokes and be the centre of a minor comedy attack, you know? You and I know many women who do this, but I think you and I know exceptional women. I don't think it's quite "correct" at some level.

Bruce McCullough

It's true that there are more women in classes [than performances], I think. I blame theatresports for that. I think it is the competition. And not that women are noncompetitive. They are. But it is real macho; it's a gladiatorial kind of comedy.

Suzanna Petzold

I think improvisation, when you take it to the performance level, has a big element of risk and letting yourself be played with as well as playing with other people. Women have to be very careful a lot of the time because they are put down and given the bitchy part to play or the baby or the mother. Not the hero, not the funny man, not the star, but always the supporting thing. I think women get tired of that—or they think that that means they're not as good, and so they tend to stay away from it.

Also, I think, in a way, women work really well as a group because we kind of look out for each other and go along slowly. Maybe, in fact, we should be better improvisors because of it. But there's a fear of taking too big a piece of cake, because a woman who takes more than her fair share is a pig and might get fat.

Rebecca Northan

Yeah, I was up at the theatre for I think a month and a half, and I was the only girl who showed up one night and I was a ten-minute player [a rookie playing in the preliminary portion of the evening]. I wasn't even captaining a ten-minute. I was afraid to, and Ron Carmichael came up and said, "We would like a girl to be in the second half. We would like a girl on our team and because there's no other girls here, we know that you aren't experienced enough, but will you please play with us just so that we have a girl on our team." And I thought, Wow, this is really scary, but I'd be really stupid to turn down this offer. I played in the second half, and if they needed a girl in the scene, I was it, but other than that I wasn't experienced enough to start scenes myself. But I got to the point where I was tired of being asked to play just because I was a girl and was treated like that for a long time, so I said, "Okay, fine. If that's what you want, I'll serve you tea and coffee in every scene." And that's all I did. In every scene I walked in and said, "Can I get you a cup of coffee?" And they should have got the message after that, but you, know . . .

I'm capable of doing more than just playing a female— being a prop. I think a lot of times girls are used as props.

I think it has something to do with the particular people and the environment because, I think it's maybe in Sweden or somewhere in Europe where it's the majority—the majority of improvisors are women, and they have a hard time getting men, so I think it definitely depends on what the society of the country is like and the personalities of the improvisors.

I think it depends on how they're treated. Because I was actually at one time invited to improvise at Jesters in the Comedy Club and was told, "We want to try using women, but in a sense we don't really need to *have* a woman in the group because it's a lot funnier for us to put on a dress and play a woman, but we'd like to try it and see what it's like, you know?" So I think it definitely depends on where you are.

Jose Roodenburg

There have been several times that I was making a joke, but just not loud enough, so a man at the table makes the same joke, and everybody is "Wow! Ah!" and I was making the joke a second before that. So I mean, on stage I find it very difficult to go for it.

Barbara Scott

I felt very lucky that when I started I was the only woman for a while but surrounded by pretty feminist men—pretty enlightened men who didn't make a big deal out of being all guys there. Things have changed radically since then. We're all women and we're run by women—our organization is run by women, more women players than men.

I think when the competition is introduced, because it seems to be inherently a male thing, that guys are raised to be good sports, and that's the focus and that's the excitement and that's what's done. Competition is such a normal part of their being raised. More and more girls are doing sports, but I don't think with the competitive edge as much as with the guys. I think when the competition comes in that it feels uncomfortable—"Oh, I don't want to have anything to do with that. I just want the fun part." Competition isn't fun. Maybe too much focus is being given to that instead of stressing that it's just a hook.

And funny women are scary. Because they tend to be bigger, not necessarily like you have to be fat to improvise, not necessarily that, but they present themselves—they have a bigger style, a bigger aura, a louder voice, and that intimidates. If I hear the word intimidates in describing me once more I will scream. When guys are funny, it's sexy. Now, I find humour very erotic—both men and women—I think Rebecca [Stockley] when she's on stage—well, off stage too—but on stage is very sexy. You know, just this marvellous aura about her, but it frightens some people because they feel that they need to be funny to have us like them, and if they're not funny, no one will like them, or they have to match that stage energy because they're not used to seeing women with that kind of big energy. I don't know. I think the more people see it, the less it will be unusual or intimidating—that horrible word.

Patti Atfield (Stiles)

In Loose Moose I think there are fewer women not only because of the training, but because of the guys in Loose Moose. When I came up with Joanne and Laura, there was a real initiation that was going on, and there was a group of guys at that time who were all single. And they would hit on you to the point where one night Joanne, Laura and I, who really didn't know each other, were in a show together, started talking and realized that we were getting the same pickup lines from the same guys. And that's when you realize what's going on, and I think that's intimidating. Or if a woman gets into a relationship with a senior improvisor and it doesn't work out or something bad happens. I think that's one reason.

I think on stage women are always being pegged into certain roles. Right, you're the wife, you're the lover, you're the girl-friend, you're the old woman, you're the sex goddess, you're the—I mean, it's very standard what you get, and because you're on a team of usually three guys and yourself, if you get a scene with say bikers picking up a chick, well, you're the chick. You know, and usually it's not even asked of you, or they don't even talk to you; you're just automatically put into that position. Or, if the scene is dying, they automatically come on to you. I think women feel very uncomfortable with that because for a long time I did, but I just decided that if that's what's need-ed, then that's what you do, kind of thing.

Dennis Cahill

We've talked about this a lot. I've heard that it's because of the nature of theatresports and because of the nature of improvisation, because even the nature of improvisation to some degree has that competitive aspect, even if it's competing with yourself in terms of—"I'm going out there, and I'm going to make it or fail." It has that competitive aspect, and some people feel that men are brought up more competitive than women, which I don't know. Some people have said they feel that because the improvisors are very aggressive, and sometimes when new women arrive at the building they are immediately—not attacked—but immediately attractive to men, that this automatically turns women off, and this may have some validity as well.

Other people have thought it's just the nature of comedy itself. Until recently there were a lot more men than women in stand-up comedy. The nature of improvisational comedy is such that having an image of yourself is important and that you are able to break down that image. Like, if you wanted to go out and play an intellectual and a goof and a coward and multiple different images, you are going to do a lot better. There's an idea that women sometimes come in with a very feminine image of themselves and they are not willing to give that up, and in comedy, to some degree, that has to be given up. I think Jan Derbyshire is one of my favourite female improvisors. You cannot pigeon-hole Jan in terms of the characters she plays. She'll play a truck driver just as likely as she'll play a housewife. But on the other hand, it doesn't sound like a reasonable theory. There's something missing from that because when you look at men improvisors, some of the men improvisors that I know are very successful and still very limited in the number of characters they play. So I'm not sure and I really don't have a solid theory of my own. I know it's a problem not just here but in many places.

It's an interesting question, and I would be interested in hearing what the women have to say about it. I've talked to some women about it, and sometimes you do get that reaction—"The guys are such jerks when you come around"— because in order to get to be an improvisor to some degree you have to be pretty outgoing and pretty assertive to actually walk out on stage and improvise. Sometimes the men that are improvisors also come on pretty strongly as personalities. Sometime they turn me off because they don't turn it off once they get off stage, and I think some women are automatically turned off by that. Who knows?

Low Status I Love You. Raymond Gurrie and Patti Atfield (Stiles). PHOTO: DEBORAH IOZZI

Ask For

FAVOURITE GAMES

We all have our favourite games for different reasons. Clem admits to having a partiality for two games. He describes his fascination with them like this:

"Word At A Time to me seems like watching two people on amphetamines walk a high wire with no net. When the game goes well it zooms about like a mad thing. No one knows where it will go, no one controls it, all you can do is ride the beast. Some of the oddest, most macabre, most outrageous scenes I have witnessed on a stage anywhere at anytime have come out of this game.

"The Hat Game holds quite a different appeal for me. It's very competitive, it is, I suppose what public contests must have been like between competing bards back in ancient days when poetry was understood by a wide body of people and not studied in universities under close scrutiny like some rare form of bacillus. Two people create a story while continually seeking to steal the other's hat. I have seen some very, very funny scenes evolve from this game and some extremely exotic methods of taking the hat. On one rare, singular occasion I have actually seen a hat removed by mouth."

Whatever the games, whatever players' reasons for favouring specific games, it's interesting to note the diversity of their appeal.

Nigel Burrows

It varies. It's progressing. Puppets [Moving Bodies] was the game, and for a while we were the only team prepared to play it. No one else in Auckland would play it. I think the first time we played it, we got three tens, and after that no one else would [play it]. Strange to see that. Now I think rhyming couplets and musical games are developing as my current favourites.

Cathleen Rootsart

Right now I like the Playbook scene where you take a play and read it. You read a page of dialogue, line for line, and only one improvisor on the stage has the script. I don't know where that came from. I think it may have been Seattle. Also, it's fun to get stories from the audience, or make up stuff like Birth of a Religion.

Frank Totino

I like to combine Status, and I think it's the most important thing to be learned from that type of improvisation as far as an actor goes. If you understand that [Status], you can understand all kinds of other stuff. If you play Status, you've got a relationship, right? And if you don't block, you've got a method of working. Then, if you start to do other things like Don't Hear [or] Hurt Yourself, it can just advance the action slowly.

I Love You scenes are among my favourites. Where you try to tell the other person you love them. I love to get set up doing that.

Vanessa Valdes

I used to like Scenes to Music, but I don't much anymore. . . . People's mime skills are pretty horrific. It frustrates me. When I put in a piece of music . . . you know, it is so easy for me to criticize when I don't do the stuff. I go, "Listen to it, listen to it! It has a very strong mood. It's got a very strong beat. I mean, you can dance to it." But when they aren't listening, it's like . . . "if you don't want any music in this mime scene, I won't put any in, but it looks like we are blocking each other with this loud music going on." So I used to like those, but not anymore.

Actually my favourite scenes are scenes where there isn't much structure. I like Word at a Time stories . . . Speaking in one Voice, He said, she said . . . those are fun. You never know where they are going to go. So I would say that my favourite scenes are the ones where they can go anywhere.

Nigel Curtain Smith

I like to do Word at a Time with a partner. I think it is the most fabulous thing when you get up into that trancey state and you are flying.

Jan Derbyshire

Starting from nothing. Going out there and having somebody throw something at you.

Kyrre Hangen Bakke

It used to be Secret Desires—the game where a common lust or obsession will emerge that is common to all the players on the stage. Nothing else is decided. I like that because I thought it was essential to impro. Because if you don't actually wait for the fish to rise, you won't catch it. I think the one I like best is the Tiny Voice scene. Once we had a scene where a young girl was contemplating suicide, and we decided to do it as the Tiny Voice, and her environment started to discuss this. I was the tree, someone else the rope and the rope said, "I don't want to be part of this." And then there's this serious discussion between the rope and the girl about the good and bad sides of suicide. As the tree, I said, "Look, I've been standing here for two hundred years, and I think it's a good idea. I mean how many times have you seen a human destroy a tree? There is a

Hat Game. Tony Totino and Graeme Davies. PHOTO: DEBORAH IOZZI

question of justice here." Then we had this argument between the girl and the rope and the tree about the philosophical aspects of suicide and the concern about the environment. I somehow felt that there was something that the audience would remember the day after.

Dave Duncan

I suppose Word at a Time is my favourite game, and I think it's the best game for teaching improvisation because no one is allowed to lead. You both must follow. You cannot push forward your own ideas. Your partner is more important than you are, and their ideas are the ones that you have to treat as important. It's a game that forces you to work in the *now* as opposed to thinking ahead. In Word at a Time you gotta think of yourself as backing through the scene so that all that you can see is what has gone on before and where you are now, and that's all you need to know. The speed that can happen and the fact that you can actually talk as fast as people do in regular conversation with two different brains working . . . I find that quite amazing, quite, ah . . . a mental achievement.

Jim McLarty

We once did an amazing Shakespearean scene. I think Vancouver is kind of known for doing style scenes like that. But we did one that was just so hot and so true to Shakespeare without a lot of the *schtick* that can go with it. We asked for two Shakespearean characters, and we got Romeo and Lady MacBeth. And we did a story of Romeo and Lady MacBeth that was . . . it could have been a plot line that He [Shakespeare] could have written about how Romeo and Lady MacBeth were good friends, and he was thanking her for always supporting him, and he, as a man of honour—if there was anything that she wanted him to do, he would do it. Well, she said, "I want you to kill Juliet." So now it's a fabulous scenario, right? He meets Juliet, he's in love with her, but he's a man of honour . . . he is bound to kill her. So he arranges to meet her the next day in the pasture, and he sets up this guy who is going to kill her with a bow and arrow when she shows up. Well, sure enough, he gets everything arranged, she shows up, but the guy slips with the bow and hits him. So Romeo dies in Juliet's arms as Lady MacBeth is cursing. I mean it was just . . . it had all the twists of a good Shakespeare scene. And, of course, it was underscored [received fewer points than it should have].

Denalda Williams

A Day in the Life, I guess. I love Day in the Life because I love watching it. I love the idea of the audience member having that fifteen minutes of fame, you know, that Andy Warhol thing, that fifteen minutes, because I think it's a high for them. And the higher they get, the higher we get.

Instead of making them Joe-who-works-at-the-7-Eleven, it's Joe-who-works-at-the-7-Eleven, but now he is speaking in Shakespearean verse. He's not just a clerk; he's a Shakespearean character. I love that.

Conny Fruhauf

I like very much the scene where one speaks in gibberish and the other translates. We often play it with Status and it's very clear. I like that.

Jochen Baum

I like Master and Servant because it shows people that status is everywhere and it can change. The master can be pulled down. That's a little, critical, social commentary, and I like that very much.

Patti Atfield (Stiles)

I love doing all the physical games. I have a really difficult time with verbal games. I have a much easier time with being physical, so things like Moving Bodies or Slow Motion Commentary or Making Faces or any of those games I really enjoy. I hate the Hat Game. I don't want to win. I just don't want to take the person's hat. I have no desire to do that, so I know that when I walk out there they are going to get the hat, and because I'm not going to try to get theirs, then it's not going to be any good for the audience so why should I be there? You know?

An Open Challenge

OTHER ROLES

As theatresports continues to evolve, it is worth reflecting that not only is the narrative improvised but the format itself is improvised—from the announcer to what in regular theatre would be called the set designer. The following accounts describe some of the less visible, but essential roles that make theatresports addictive.

THE ANNOUNCER

John Gilchrist

Somewhere over the fall of '79 when theatresports was forming, there were a lot of gaps on stage—a lot of different players at different levels—and Keith came up with the idea that it would be good to have a commentator [now called the announcer], or someone doing a bit of narration to help keep the flow going—occasionally abusing the judges and making them adhere to the rules, and helping out the actors as little as possible.

So I was about the only person that wasn't on stage at the time, and actually the first person to do this particular role was Frank Totino. He did it for a week or two, and then, of course, it was more important that he be on stage. So I said, "What the heck, let me give it a shot here." So I became the commentator. That was some time in the fall of '79, and that carried all the way through until I left in '84.

Also, I guess over that time period my contribution to it, aside from trying to arrange tournaments and keep people together and what not, was in helping formalize some of the rules . . . not so much in the performance rules, but insofar as timing and points went and how theatresports was scored and things like that.

So I helped, we would try something one night, it wouldn't work, so we would throw out that rule and make another rule. But I tried to keep track of the mathematical necessities of theatresports scoring. That sort of fell onto me, and I took care of that. We had an incredibly complex system of scoring for a long while until we decided it was too much effort, and it's been toned down since then. Sometimes it's up to the commentator and the sound improvisor to fill in—it is very easy to appear disjointed when you are doing theatresports because it is a very disjointed thing. So I think that I always felt that the Commentator helped fill the flow between a good scene and a bad one. On a good night, you know, maybe you would say twenty words. On a bad night, you know, you were sweating to death.

SOUND IMPROVISOR

Vanessa Valdes

I remember once, they all came up to me and said, "Vanessa, we would like for you to try sound next weekend." There were these sort of formalities like—Who wants to do sound? Who wants to do . . . It was like an audition.

I remember that night so well because, first of all, when I started doing sound it was so time-consuming because I didn't really know the tapes—I didn't have any tapes of my own—and the tapes, they were just tapes. They had nothing listed on what they were, so you would sit and listen through the whole bloody tape. And you'd think, Mm, I guess this sounds kind of scary. Well, maybe there is something better on the other side. It would take me between five and six hours to cue for a show.

Now, if I've done the show the week before, it will take me

an hour because physically I have so many tapes now, it takes me time to lay them out. In the old days I would have fifty or sixty tapes. Now I have four hundred or plus. I know those tapes so well now.

So the first show I was really lucky. They showed me how they set out the tapes—you'd cue a tape to a specific place of music or sound effect. You'd lay it out of the box so that you could get to it really quick. It's no good if it takes you five minutes because the scene will be over.

Vanessa Valdes – Goddess of Sound. PHOTO: DEBORAH IOZZI

I remember the first night. I was nervous. Anyways, I started it up—and it used to be "The March" by Mancini that got the opening of the show started, and that was the only scripted part. Okay, I didn't fuck it up. I remember the scene. It was Donna Raddick and Maggie Matulic. She was a dance instructor and Donna was this pupil. She goes, "Okay, one and two and three," and I had some Chopin in there. I remember going [she screams], and I looked down on the benches—it was either Rick [Hilton] or Dave [Duncan]—and they went, "All right!" and I went, "Oh, I just did it."

It was a major revelation. I can really help something like that, and it's not that hard. I just have to concentrate on what I'm seeing and wait for it because, you know, it's all timing. I remember that night was the biggest buzz I had ever had! I mean, I remember not going home. I went out with some people after for something to eat, and this was just like the most exciting thing I had ever done. It was great.

Then came the time when I started doing more and more because the people that were doing sound, like Rick and Dave, were saying that they wanted to improvise. They didn't want to do sound. So there were a couple of years when I was the only person doing it up there.

There are the noncreative aspects of the job. You have the sound that starts the show up, whatever piece it is. For something like theatresports, you put in scene change music—after a scene ends, before another scene begins, well, there is really dead space. If they get a title, let's say "Sixteen Candles," then I will try to find something with a sixteen at the end of the scene to, you know, bridge. And then there is just winging it, you know, putting on music and they have to improvise to the music that you are using. And then, the most fun, I think, is if you can get it spot on, the kind of music that the environment needs, or just to mold a scene, get a scene going forward or bring a scene to its natural end, you know, just to make a nice package. That's always the best time.

THE SCENOGRAPHER

Shawn Kinley

Originally I think Dennis [Cahill] asked Tom Lamb and I to help out backstage bringing out beds or sofas and help move things more quickly during the Theatresports Tournament of the Olympics in 1988. It turned out to be such an interesting idea, a good thing to have for the performers. I mostly perform, make money doing mime and my voice isn't that well developed so sometimes I feel uncomfortable talking. I do a lot of mask making, mask performing. I thought this idea of improvising backstage would be a chance to be on stage with a different purpose, tune my skills but not have the performance pressure. So for me that was a good way to start. For Dennis, I think it was a way to make things a little easier for the performers.

Scenography has branched out beyond just helping the performers, it's something to add colour and depth to the show. A scenographer by definition should set scenes, colour the stage. It's more than putting a chair on the stage and saying, "Here we are in the throne room." You should be able to set the atmosphere by adding a flag and a couple of guards. Scenography has evolved from just being asked by the director or performers to bring out a chair, to the scenographers initiating scenes. We have set out scenography on the stage before the performers have had a chance to set anything up themselves. Keith says it helps the performers by not having to go to the audience for suggestions all the time, and it throws them into an unexpected situation.

We also react to whatever the performers are doing on stage as well. So if the performers are driving in a car, we've pushed the fake car out there for them. And instead of just letting them sit there pretending to move, we're out there with trees or cows or something making it look like they are passing things as they drive along. You know, carrying things by them, floating people through space, stuff like that.

We have a whole pamphlet on what a scenographer should be or shouldn't be. You shouldn't be up on stage trying to hog it or throwing on a toilet seat because you think it's funny. You have to do things that support the performers and make them look good. Then you've done your job. If you're working to make yourself look good and get a laugh then you've failed. But sometimes when you're sitting backstage, it gets kinda boring, so you try a gag now and then. But we learn from those and try not to do too many. One of the major failures of scenography is that few theatres that do theatresports have their own theatres or a backstage full of props like we do at Loose Moose. Not many theatres have the means to try it.

There have been moments where you know you've really done it right and been really appreciated by the audience and the performers. One of those moments was setting up Old Rome. We had pillars that look like marble and plants everywhere. I was draped in a kind of classical-looking way as a Roman statue standing on a pedestal peeing into a bucket, uh, with a squirt bottle thing, of course. And it looked really nice, and the whole scene had this sound of the fountain running through it. The scenography was funny and the scene went really well too. So everything worked hand in hand.

Another time Kathleen Foreman was on stage singing and supposedly she had a voice that could kill. There were two glasses on the stage and I ran out and broke them while she was singing and it added to the scene. Yeah, those kind of moments.

THE COMPERE (AUSTRALIA)

Lyn Pierse

The compere is a particular style that comes from our Tivoli tradition based on the British musical tradition. It is get up and do your gig, like a series of stand-ups. Australia has a wonderful history of that. It is straight from the *commedia*—there is no doubt about it. Its roots are back there, and it is Pantomime as well.

Our first compere was Paul Chubb. He is a very big man, and he is very loved in the Australian industry. He is as warm and as respected as Jack Lemon and as loved as Art Carney. He compered with this "I don't know what the hell is going on. Do you?" attitude. The first night coming to this thing, he didn't know what he was going to do. Nobody knew what they were going to do. A sellout audience and thirty-five of us on stage with a musician we had never met before with all this stuff on stage. This set turned up with all the games on it, and the audience is screaming and the lights start flicking; the whistles are going and the audience is screaming! I run on as timekeeper, then the musician and then the compere. And Paul goes, "Good evening and welcome to theatresports," and the audience goes absolutely crazy.

THE ADMINISTRATOR (LONDON)

Melanie Miller

When I saw theatresports, it had an instant attraction for me because people enjoyed it so much. It is a very good program, and there is lots of potential. I have been a manager and have had lots of staff training, and I found improvisation quite fascinating. The philosophy behind it attracted me because the structure was simple but yet wouldn't allow anyone to abuse it. Because of the team spirit, people became very protective of the game structure. I was hoping to set up an administration structure that mirrored the playing structure. I renamed a lot of the administration terminology so that the players could relate to it.

There are two of us who have managed to get the London group going. We see ourselves as a group that will help other people in the UK set up their own groups. Maybe they will learn from our mistakes. I must spend about seventy per cent of my time dealing with the politics of who gets to do what. I think it would be a good idea if Keith or Loose Moose said, "Here's your constitution, here's your rules and this is how you set yourself up." Then people would have a certain structure that they would accept. We have wasted so much time trying to work that out ourselves. We've gone through about four structures. Now we've got the present one, which is by no means perfect, but it's a structure.

Keith always comes up with the right answers for me. He is always very easy and clear. He has a broad perspective on everything that's going on. He is like big daddy; he holds our hand. Of our top improvisors, there are people who disagree with the way that he does things and some of his theories. But when you meet him, he doesn't set down laws. Everything is open to interpretation and change. He is very open to other means, which is great, but it doesn't help people when they are struggling to start out. Because you need rules so you can learn them. And learn when to break from them.

Advancing the Action

THE FUTURE OF THEATRESPORTS

And where lies the future of theatresports? Like the game itself, this question stirs up a broad range of opinions and feelings.

Gary Campbell

I'd like it to get a little bit more organized than it is right now—so that the survival is ensured. I think here in Toronto it is doubtful that it would ever fade away. But it could because the organization just sort of comes and goes. And people's interest in it waxes and wanes. I would like it to not become much more than it is. Just better organized. Have it there for people to do what so many people have done in the past twelve years, which is be able to come off the street or to come out of your high school or out of your workshop and hit a stage and learn about improvising. Just learn in that format that is theatresports how to improvise. Are you an improvisor? Learn all those things slowly and safely at theatresports. Let it be a gentle, almost socially oriented thing. Because that is something that we haven't mentioned, that theatresports has always been a social thing. I mean, a real social thing. You get into theatresports, and that becomes your circle of friends as well. There is a theatre community, but there is also a *theatresports community*, and it is huge. And it lasts, it endures. I mean, oh yeah, my oldest friends are theatresports friends.

Bruce McCullough

You know, it is really interesting to me that it is so big in Europe and that it hasn't quite taken off in New York where I thought it would really take off. I mean, they are sort of still struggling, don't you think? And they have worked really hard here [in Toronto] to keep it going. I don't think it has been the run away success here I had envisioned. I don't know about the future of it. I mean, it is nice to be optimistic about it, but it is hard. By nature it is about turnover, it seems. Some people have been doing it for a number of years, but I think it's like—you [Kathleen Foreman and Clem Martini] probably know yourself—when you go to Loose Moose to see theatresports, there are so many faces that are new to you.

It is a young person's game. Or a young performer's game, and I think its future is always bright because people always want to perform, and that's the best part about it, and it is in a way the worst part. Because I think the theatre community, which I also love, learns from itself. And a writer writes a good play and a bad play, but generally there is some crap. There is also some crap in theatresports, but I don't know what an artist looks like after playing theatresports for twenty years.

Mark McKinney

Theatresports is played for lots of different reasons. I mean, I shouldn't point the finger and say that people get into it just to get into Second City, but a lot of people do that, you know. They see the *Kids in the Hall* being successful, and people move on through Second City and Mike Meyers and all this sort of stuff. It worries me when I see people skipping a step, you know, and not actually learning how to improvise. Nobody really passionately cares if they're fucking up, but I just realize how vital it was for me as a performer and as a writer. When you're relaxed and open-minded, you're a much better actor, and in the same sense it can apply to writing.

George Babiak

It's just very exciting to be part of a group that is international in scope. And we have been talking about forming an institute. I don't know what is going to happen, but it is moving in that direction. So there will be some kind of body that oversees everything and monitors what's going on all over the place.

Frank Totino

From what I understand, it is still growing. It is spreading around the world. People are enjoying it, audiences go to it. It attracts performers.

I don't have that much to do with it anymore. I rarely play it. What it is, is growing really big, and I think it will keep going.

But what it looks like to me now is that the audiences all seem to be within a certain age group. The audiences don't grow up. The only thing that gets older is the performers. The guys who stay in it. The audiences stay young—high school and younger. And I think that is a result of it becoming just funny. Just funny.

You see the audiences laughing like crazy at it because it's not very hard to make a twenty-year-old laugh. All you've got to do is just be stupid and they'll laugh, you know. And at the same time it is very difficult to get into any other kind of topic, other than dating and school and going for burgers or whatever. Watching television. You can't really talk about anything else. So improvising is fun, and we all (us old guys) still do it in spite of the fact that all we can do is make young kids laugh. There is nothing terribly wrong about that.

Vanessa Valdes

I would like it to get to a professional level—like the tennis players' have a pro circuit. You know, where you have a good group, a very good group of improvisors from all over the place that would go on these extended tours and do workshops. Sort of like what happened in New Zealand. I mean, I think the country got a lot out of that tour.

I would like to see regular tournaments. International tournaments. Not really for the tournament's sake but for the educational sake. I think the school [the International Improvisation School run out of Calgary] is a very exciting development. I think we have to be very careful. Keith has to be really careful that we don't lose this baby. Because the potential of it becoming very boring and really safe . . . is very strong. I mean, you have got to keep an eye on where it's going. You guys [the original Loose Moose improvisors] didn't start it and work all these years to have it turn into a . . . yucca, yucca, yucca. You know, stand-up comedian, sort of . . . Shriner's convention.

Randy Dixon

Well, I'd like to make a little more money at it. I think that every improvisor's fantasy is to just constantly do it, you know? I really like what's happening now, internationally, all these little pockets of people tied into one another. Talking about theatresports worldwide, I would like to see lots more exchanges, tournaments, workshops. Have someone come to Seattle for five or six months. Live in New York or somewhere for a few months and do it. I've done that a few times and it's been great. I think we should be pushing the form, trying out different adaptations, like this soap opera thing we're doing. Taking improv and putting it into another form.

Rebecca Stockley

One of my immediate dreams is our own space where we can have offices and teach classes and have shows. For the cities that have their own theatre, I see so much happen for them when they get that. For one thing, you can develop an audience if you're not a gypsy. I would just love to see theatresports in high schools all over the place. You know, as much as it's just a silly thing, it's also great for self-esteem for young people. In the inner cities, students don't have anything that really interests them in school, and if there were a theatresports team in these schools, then the kids would have some place to go and hang out that isn't a street corner. So as corny as that might sound, I do think that it could make the world a better place if there were theatresports in every high school in the city.

From my experience, the world has opened up to me through theatresports because of these experiences of going to tournaments and that sort of thing. It's this tremendous network internationally, and I've met people that I never would have had anything in common with, people from other lands that I wouldn't have been able to speak to, but because we have theatresports in common, we're friends.

Barbara Scott

I love this stuff. It's a marvellous opportunity for anyone who wants to be in a community. It's a big, big family. It's like in Greece—if you know how to dance, you're in. It's a great time 'cause you can just go to a city and say, "I'm an improvisor," and people go, "Yeahhh, come on in!"

Nigel Curtain Smith

Theatresports is a great contributor to the Global Village notion. There's going to be much more travel involved than anyone ever thought. I'm very staunchly, strongly a Tasmanian, and I think that my immediate aim would be to tie up some loose ends in southeast Australia. I would like to see more tournament things happen to bring things closer together, and in a sense that is happening. We should see an Australian national circuit.

Call it in the Air

L–R: Patti Atfield (Stiles), Ron Carmichael, Raymond Gurrie
PHOTO: DEBORAH IOZZI

Patti Atfield (Stiles)

I think theatresports itself is at a breaking point right now. I think it's either going to go gungho and become much more popular and it'll be a household word or it's going to start deteriorating. I think it's at the level right now that those people I keep speaking of who have learned from Keith and were in the initial stage are either starting to get bored with it or starting to look for new areas to challenge themselves or wandering away. And the next level that's coming in doesn't have whatever that thing I keep talking about is. I don't know if it's a lack of training or what. Companies like Toronto and Edmonton and Vancouver are still developing and still creating things for performance. They're not creating things for technique and development. So everything that they do is for the benefit of the audience instead of for the benefit of their own training.

Michael Sanderson-Green

Something that I would like to see happen again is the TV series from Sydney. They had teams from all over the country. We still get audience members that say they've seen it on TV, and that's all they know about it. Publicity from that was enormous.

Ellen Idelson

My dream is that we have our own theatre—with space to perform in and offices that we could pay for with the work that we do. That we become and continue as a mainstay of Los Angeles theatre and, you know, be recognized for the unique quality that theatresports has. I do think that theatresports has provided an oasis for a lot of people who are fed up with the rat race in LA. It is a tool for people to put into their everyday lives, especially in such a hectic environment.

Paul Bernardo

I think that the thing will continue to expand; it will continue to grow. I think you may even see centres like what is happening in Washington, DC, where you have two organizations in the same metropolis doing theatresports. I mean, now what happened is that you've the Improv Olympics, which is some guy who is doing the same thing but not calling [it theatresports], changing it slightly because he couldn't get the rights to the name or whatever. So you've got some corporate reasons that might keep theatresports from spreading the way it has. But I think it is going to end up all over the world. At some point, it would be interesting if Calgary and Keith Johnstone could convince the Canadian government how big it is so that they could get funding enough so that they could be the umbrella organisation to tie it all together.

Mel Tonken

My sense of it is that if it was going to catch on in a big way, it would have done so by now.

Patricia Ryan Madson

I'd like to see all of us who care about this work keep doing it in our own way. I think that the beginning has been healthy. We can't be Keith, but we can, I think, somehow keep the spirit of the work alive no matter how we transform it.

I think it's important and I think the international schools are important for the movement for a couple of reasons. I see it as a movement in the sense that you've got a philosophy, a new paradigm—because you can talk about "Keith's Work," his creation of theatresports as an art form, his development of an educational model for teaching improv and creativity. Let's call this whole thing a paradigm for a moment. When someone's created a paradigm, it's important to make a pilgrimage to the home of the founder. There's something about his being the creator of this work, the founder of it, that commands respect. To go to the foot of the mountain of the leader is important, and I think that for people around the world to come to Calgary to pay homage to him—he'd hate this, he'd hate me saying this—but it's important that people come to where this form was born and see him there.

So from the spiritual perspective, "You go to the guru's place." You have to take a journey to get there. That's important. I think it's really important that people from all over the world rub elbows with each other. The international character of the work and the fact that he has flown all over the globe giving his work away to the world and allowing us to feel that network by rubbing arms with an Italian and a Swede and an Australian or whatever is very important . . . because I think this work is changing the world and part of it is that it is international in character. And there'll be a time when Keith either won't be alive or won't be running things so that the people who are interested in the work around the world need to know each other. So from the practical point of view, logistically touching hands across the sea is more than just a kind of courtesy. I think it's essential.

Cathleen Rootsart

I don't know what the future is. It's strange because there was a time when I would have had an answer for you directly, when I would have felt personally tied to theatresports. I think everybody goes through a phase when they become intensely . . . theatresports, theatresports! I mean, you play it and think about it and it's what you do. I was the sort of administrator, artistic director for a while and felt feverish about it, but I don't know that I do anymore. I think theatresports is really fun to do. It's been really important in my personal development. The international tournaments are so much fun and that sort of sharing with people is really valuable. Then when you go and play in individual people's leagues, I think that you kind of realize and say, "They sometimes have houses (attendance) of thirty and fifty people as well." And it's not this huge, glorious thing that it is when you all get together, you know? It's so big, yet in many ways it's very small. I mean, I'm surprised that it hasn't really taken off, you know? I know people that are more familiar with Comedy Sports in the States.

Michael Gregory

In five years time I would like to see a greater variety of shows. There's a kind of speed and agility about theatresports' star performers, which applies heavily to comedy. Basically theatresports says to an audience, "You will laugh. Occasionally you may feel sad or cry or see a serious scene." It would be nice to create a show which is a little bit more serious, where the audience will laugh as well. I mean, some of the most serious scenes are hilarious.

John Gilchrist

One of the great things about theatresports is the openness of it, and the way that if groups treat it right, it can develop new people. For a lot of people starting off in theatre, people who have passed through theatresports at one time or another, it's been good.

I don't think it has had a lot of effect on the formal writers and producers and directors of theatre. No, I could be wrong. If anything, I think it has had an effect on the actors and perhaps some of the directors on how they approach a script—that they are willing to look at an improvisational way of getting to a point rather than just to keep repeating it.

So many people have tried to pooh-pooh theatresports for so long from the formalized side of theatre, it's almost like two camps. I think when we see more new play workshops and in situations like that, where more impro can come into it, I think it can have a big effect.

Veena Sood

Well, there's *its* vision and then *your* vision. Its vision . . . I think its become a worldwide thing. And Keith has become well known as a result of it. And if I name drop Keith as my teacher, it looks good. But my personal vision of it . . . for me . . . fitting into it. I thought it would be bigger. I would be on television and famous and making much more money. And I can't do that as an improvisor so I've had to go off and do that as an actor.

Kathy Destephano

I wanted to say something else. We also believe that it's time for a change in theatre as it is. Just our personal opinion at our place in Rotterdam. A lot of theatre is stale. There is very little improvisation in Holland, to my knowledge. And if there is, it is usually imported. It is usually people coming in from other . . . yeah, Americans, English.

So what I am interested in doing is to set up an improvisational centre in Rotterdam. Because Rotterdam is screaming for fresh forms of theatre, and there are lots of subsidies there. Like in many European countries, it is just so different from here [Calgary].

So my plan is to set up an organization that can teach theatresports techniques and to train the teams. I hope to have a strong theatresports team and a strong organization that can meet everyone's needs who wants to get involved with theatresports in Holland.

And one last thing that I think is inevitable is this TV thing. Finding a way to do it on TV. And then to see how that will bring theatresports to all kinds of people who wouldn't normally get it so that it goes into the community and you have schools competing and community centres competing.

In Holland, the amateur theatre is highly subsidized and very popular so that is a very interesting challenge to see if that can be combined.

Tony Totino

I think the future of theatresports is . . . well, it doesn't have such a great future particularly if the centre, if Keith's theatre company in Calgary, doesn't find a way of going to all the different places that do theatresports and presenting themselves as the experts and the founders of theatresports. I don't know if this is any kind of an analogy. . . . Martha Graham, the modern dancer, right? If nobody had ever been able to see her dances on film or go to New York to see her company, if her work had sort of spread out without examples *visually* of her style and technique, what would her technique of dancing look like now? I think it would be really bizarre and unconnected to the centre and incorrect . . . and I think that's what's happening to theatresports, and that's what's going to happen to theatresports unless some artistic control or at least artistic example is set from the centre because the show drifts further and further into mundane madness every year. You know, the groups don't necessarily get better; they get more banal.

One of the things that Keith and the Loose Moose Theatre Company ought to try to find is a way to correct this thing about making the game "fair." I mean, what's fair? Why on earth should things be fair? It's a *staged show!* I mean, you don't go around giving a few extra lines to Laertes because he doesn't have as many lines as Hamlet. There's this mistaken idea that it should be fair, it should be fun, it should be all these different things. It tends to make it into some kind of sophomoric game show. The biggest problem facing theatresports is the fact that groups doing it have no example from which to work, and because of that, they end up looking thin and uninteresting.

Lyn Pierse

The other place that we've got to get is Russia. When we can start playing Russia, that will be sensational. If we can get a team from New Zealand, Australia, Russia, Canada, we can get a sort of world focus. I want to take the Australian government for a workshop. That might be nice.

And we should remember, no matter how we differ, we all play the same game. Isn't that true? That is the one thing about Australians—they do all play the same games. There is a link between all of us, no matter how fine we get to nearly killing each other. Now three of the Australian centres, who were at first financially linked to the Belvoir franchising network, and all of New Zealand, have asked to have direct commitment to Canada. And the rest of Australia plays through the theatre company where I am. And what is happening now is that the Australian centres are coming back together now through an artistic commitment through our schools programs, which are very good. It's working in every state. I am very proud of it. We want to keep what Keith talks about—the purity. Just take the things that are relevant to us and still continue to play in a way that somehow fits our culture.

It is not theatre; it is theatre sport. It is an international league. I'm in that club. Like if you are in the Catholic Church, then you put money into the church.

John Poulsen

I really believe that Johnstone—this is going to sound like John Lennon's "More Important Than Christ" line—but I think Johnstone is influencing theatre today far more than almost anybody. If only because people who have been Keith Johnstone's . . . protégés, I guess, for lack of a better word . . . are now out in the theatre, doing theatre, and they have a theatresports background. And they want to have that same feeling, that same kick, that same power. And one thing theatresports does usually have is a good pace, nice intensity and very often an honesty that regional theatre . . . it's not that regional theatre rarely has it. It's just that they can have poor pace, they can have poor characterization, they can have a lack of honesty and they can still sell tickets. But in theatresports, generally if you don't have that, you are off the stage pretty quickly, I'd say. So it teaches you.

Rebecca Northan

I don't know. I sometimes think that theatresports will never die, that it will always have some kind of an audience and there will always be people willing to play it, but I hope that the shows improve. Right now I think that over the past little while theatresports hasn't been as fun to me as it used to be. I don't know what the future of theatresports is. I mean, I think there are some people who want it to be on TV, but I don't think it really works on film because even when you watch theatresports live, if it's good, if the show is really hot, people don't believe that you are really improvising. If you put it on film, there's no way people are going to believe it's improvised, "Oh, they must have scripted this; they took hours to film this," and if it's bad they'll say, "Why would they ever put anything this stupid on TV? This is terrible."

Rick Hilton

In many ways I'm really disappointed by it. Because in the early stages I thought it was going to be like a breakthrough in all theatre. It would become not only like mainstream theatre, but it would . . . *change* theatre. And it certainly has not done that. It's still on the perimeter of theatre, on the outskirts of traditional theatre.

So it hasn't broken in like I thought it was going to and become a new theatre. I don't know that it ever will. Once Keith stopped being involved in it, he made a conscious decision at some point that that was it. He was going to let it run. Never even told us that. I think that is when the real evolution kind of reached its peak. The exciting evolution. We are still playing a similar game; we are just more skilled at it. We can see when the mistakes are happening a little bit quicker.

Veena Sood

I find that I keep thinking that I'm too old for it. I don't like getting down on my knees; they hurt. I can't jump around as much as I used to . . . and I don't want to. I don't want to be fast and loud. I want to be slow and calm, and theatresports doesn't want you to be slow and calm. It doesn't make you think you *can*.

Dennis Cahill

Some days I think theatresports is going to continue to spread. There'll be more sort of interchange and exchange between different groups, and it'll be a wonderful and glorious thing. It will all make us better and make the world a brighter and happier place to live. Some days I feel that way.

Some days I wake up and think, I'm really sick of theatresports. When I go to tournaments, I'm bored. I'm sometimes frustrated because the quality of improvisation seems to reach a certain point and then totally die off. People seem more interested in succeeding as performers rather than exploring the possibilities of improvisation, and I find that very frustrating. And I think if theatresports disappeared off the face of the earth tomorrow that would be just fine with me.

So usually I'm probably somewhere in between. I think theatresports will continue to spread. It seems to spread somewhat on its own—people seem to hear about it or they see a performance or they take a workshop, and it seems to spread.

I'm sure there will be international competitions or tournaments, which are quite often very nice in terms of being able to meet other people and make contacts. It's interesting that some of the groups that have been playing theatresports for years now are not commercially successful, and in a way that makes them stale. Other groups are extremely successful, and that seems to get them into a rut in that they have a set product that sells well and they do not want to change it, they do not want to improve it. They become very *schtick* oriented.

To me, theatresports should be just another step towards experimenting with improvisation, and now it's just another thing that we do—albeit, it's a very successful thing, but I would hope that what it does is get people to look at other ways to improvise. It's not just the end product. And I feel sometimes that's how people look at it.

A couple of years ago, Keith started playing with the idea of serious theatresports, and though it never went anywhere, the idea intrigued me because theatresports is usually, if not always, comedy based. The idea of actually having to play serious theatresports forces you as a performer, as an improvisor, to do something different. But if there wasn't something to do with Keith or Keith's influence sort of nudging or pushing us towards that, I might have quit a long time ago because it becomes sort of boring.

Anne Marie Broekhuizen

Well, we tried in Holland to keep on, connect with the cities and to set up a national organization. That didn't work out. There was too much competition. Everybody wants to be the expert. It is quite an easy situation here [in Calgary]. It is clear that Keith is the expert, and that when Keith is not here, Dennis is the expert. And it is nice to have a coach. But that is not the situation in Holland. I think we won't get that situation also. So we continue and develop the theatresports teams in the different cities, and we need each other anyhow. So we will continue to work, to work together. And organize workshops together, and we invite our other cities' teams to join in the workshops. But I would really like to, for Utrecht, that we could establish more as a group, that we could settle down in a theatre. I find the last two years very hard to continually feed the group with training sessions and organizing the shows.

Barry Cook

Interesting. In England, one of the reasons I stepped away from it was because it was becoming more cabaret, like . . . more stand-up comedy. People out to be funny. Less stories being told. Let's get on to the next gag. And having seen this in Vancouver as well, I would say that possibly by its very nature, theatresports depends on the character of its audience. If what you get from them is that they want cabaret, then they will get cabaret. It is possible that the audience may want something else, but I think the group must show the audience, and the performers, that *more* is possible. I think that theatresports will continue to be popular but perhaps mutate into something that not even Keith (and his twisted sense of humour) could have planned for.

Veena Sood

On the good side, here in Vancouver, you can virtually—well, up until six months ago—some people were virtually making a full-time living. We entertain at very highbrow corporate functions. We get flown all over the world to do twenty-minute shows.

Rick Hilton

We have this easily transportable, successful show that may not be the most artistic . . .

Veena Sood

In some ways, this is actually better. I like it that we are taking this into IBM sales people's minds, and . . . you know . . . big-time business people who have absolutely no idea about it, but all *want* to be able to think that way. I like how the school system is buying into it, finally, ten years later. They use theatresports as a model of thinking to help redo this entire curriculum. We went to various conventions and principals' and teachers' meetings. We were doing shows and workshops, and they all came to us and said, "This is exactly the kind of thinking that we want our students to have." You know, the Don't Block kind of attitude.

Rick Hilton

Accept the failure. The failure teaches you.

Veena Sood

Fail willingly and happily. Every idea is a good idea, and chances are the good ideas are the first ideas—all this sort of style of thinking. They finally bought into it. They don't think of us as the bad kids anymore. The revolutionary street punks that are going to fuck you. So maybe the revolution has succeeded.

Rick Hilton

Quiet revolution.

Glossary of Terms

THEATRESPORTS TERMINOLOGY
AROUND THE WORLD

In an effort to collect the language of theatresports as it has evolved throughout the world, we asked for submissions of terminology from the various companies. The following terms, specific to theatresports, that are referred to throughout the interviews. A few terms are used only in the locations from which they originated.

From the *Schools Manual,* United Schools Theatresports, New Zealand

*Accepting: In order for a scene to advance, offers—either physical or verbal—must be *accepted*. An offer can be *accepted* in many ways: through the naming of, reacting to, physical contact with or advancing of another player's idea. It is important that all offers are *accepted* in an affirmative way.

*Advancing: When you *advance* on an offer, you build on one idea and take it forward to the next connected idea or event. *Advancing* is simply taking the next logical step in a chain of events from which a story will be created.

Ask For: This refers to the wording used to elicit a suggestion from the audience that the players will then use as an integral part of their story. The manner in which the *ask for* is phrased can help to ensure that a specific suggestion is received (e.g. a "non-geographical location" will lead to a suggestion of "bakery" before "Malta").

Blocking: Players *block* an offer when they do not accept and incorporate another teammate's idea into the story. *Blocking* often indicates that one player is driving the scene with little or no regard for teammates' input. Saying "no" is often an indication of *blocking* and ultimately will prevent a story from advancing.

Breaking the Routine: A player begins a story by establishing an activity, or *routine*—washing the dishes, for instance. At some point, to maintain audience interest and develop the story, this *routine* will have to be broken, usually through some related activity. In the case of washing dishes, a plate could be broken, the taps may refuse to shut off or a secret code could be discovered in the bottom of a bowl.

Challenge: A *challenge* is a call to create a story issued to a team by its opponents or by the M.C. Whatever story they present, it must in some way meet the conditions of the *challenge*. A *challenge* can be broad ("A story about hunting"), specific ("A story about a prince who couldn't speak") or a United Theatresports game. A *challenge* can only be turned aside on a decision by the M.C. or the judges.

Commenting: To *comment* is to step outside the story and make an observation about it. This removes the players and the audience from the story that has been created. Once the reality of the scene has been destroyed in this way, it is often difficult to return to the story and advance it.

Complementary Offer: To make a *complementary offer* is to enter a story with an idea that will add to and advance what is already onstage. If a teammate is onstage painting, another player should avoid duplicating that action and instead offer something which will complement it, such as stirring a new can of paint. This presents a new offer to advance upon.

Crossover: A *crossover* is a brief contribution that a player makes to another team's story. The purpose is to enhance the story or assist the other team in some way and thereby create a better show. *Crossovers* often flesh out environments (e.g. two doctors walk past a crowded emergency room talking about their golf game) or advance an offer within the story (e.g. A player says, "Gee, the stores are busy at Christmas," and players from other teams take on the roles of harried seasonal shoppers). *Crossovers* are the best possible example of the philosophy that the quality of the show comes before winning and losing.

Endowing: When a teammate greets a player at the door as "Auntie Sam," this players has been *endowed* with a familial relationship. He or she must accept this as the truth and incorporate that *endowment* into his or her character and story. An improvised story is made up of an endless series of *endowments.*

Extending: To *extend* is to focus in on one idea and explore all aspects of it until that idea is then advanced upon. By *extending*, characters are fleshed out and made familiar, relationships are explored, objects are made to seem real and the audience is able to feel a part of the story.

Focus: Focus is the line of clarity in a story. Whichever player has the audience's attention at any given moment has *focus*. When there are too many players onstage, *focus* is easily lost and confusion may result. All players need to give and take *focus* as required in the telling of the story.

*Forfeit: This is the judges' call used in Christchurch to penalize a player for some infraction during a scene. This can be a block, a wimp, a sexist or racist remark or action, and so on. The judge can then hand out a specific limitation for the next scene a player does. (e.g. He or she must play with hands tied behind his or her back and speak in rhyming couplets.)

*Gagging: Gagging is taking commenting one step further. In this instance, the player steps outside the story to go for a

cheap laugh. This effectively undermines the other players and implies a lack of commitment to the story.

Gibberish: *Gibberish* is a made-up language. Although nonsensical in its sound, each phrase a player utters should have a meaning. "Ugawishwa" could mean "Hello" or "Are you hungry?" All those who speak the language are able to understand one another.

Joker: Auckland occasionally includes a guest improvisor that each team must use at least once during the evening and sometimes in very specific ways. On one occasion, for example, the M.C.—when cued by an actor—called out "Joker," freezing the action in the scene. The Joker then contributed an offer that was meant to change the direction of the story.

Naming: When a location, person or object presents itself in your story, you *name* it so that everyone knows exactly where you are, who you are with and what object you are dealing with.

Narrative: The *narrative* is the storyline of the scene. A scene with strong *narrative* will have a clear beginning, middle and end.

Offering: *Offers* are the building blocks of good improvisation. To make an *offer* and have it accepted is to allow an idea to grow into a story. An *offer* changes a story—taking it in another direction or simply adding to what has already been established.

Pointless Originality: *Pointless originality* is the introduction of an idea that comes out of nowhere and is so farfetched that it has no grounding in the reality of the story. Instead of making the next logical offer, the player takes the story too far too fast and deprives the scene of its natural growth.

Reincorporation: An offer is explored and then put aside. The story advances without it. At some point, this offer is *reincorporated,* or reintroduced by a player, tying a "forgotten" element back into the story. This is a satisfying experience for both the players and the audience because it creates a unified story with all loose ends tied up.

Shelving: Reincorporation cannot take place without *shelving.* A player *shelves* an offer when he or she puts it to one side. The story now advances without it. All players have the option of reincorporating this offer later in the story, or they may choose to leave it *shelved.*

Spontaneity: *Spontaneity* refers to the state of players in the present moment without any preconceptions or external constraints. It is a state of being that allows an unrestrained flow of ideas.

Wimping: To *wimp* is to accept an offer but not to advance upon it. Phrases like "I don't know" and "Maybe" are good examples of *wimping.* The player is not blocking, but he or she is also not taking responsibility for the forward action of the story.

AUSTRALIA SUBMISSIONS

From the forthcoming publication *Theatresports Down Under: A Guide for Coaches and Players* by Lyn Pierse, notes compiled and edited by Tania Bulmer, Sydney: Improcorp, 1994.

The People

M.C. Compere, Referee: The host of a theatresports evening, liasing between the audience, teams and crew.

Timekeeper: A performing stage manager, responsible for recording team scores, timing games and giving specific calls for teams (e.g. slow motion, ten years later, inner sing, etc.)

Mr. Music: Onstage musician, performing live, improvised music. Mr. Music extends teams' offers and adds atmosphere to the scenes. He or she is seen as a fifth team member.

The Hanging Judge: A technique judge with the power to stop a disastrous impro by honking or giving the "gong."

Beginner-Beginners: Theatresports novices in their first term of training.

Beginners: They were Beginner-Beginners. Now they're Beginners beginning their second term of training.

Intermediates: In the beginning, they were beginner-beginners, then they began Beginners, and now they have begun Intermediates.

Veterans and Advanced Players: Veterans, or "vets," are players who began at the absolute beginning and now have begun a session for themselves. Advanced players are players who weren't there at the beginning but began well and because of it have begun with the vets.

Note
Vets don't train; they "jam."
Intermediates don't jam; they "rehearse."
Beginners don't rehearse; they "train."
Players don't train; they "workshop."
Teams don't workshop; they have "coffee."

Novelties

The Gong: A small horn used by the hanging judge to remove those "painful-to-watch" impros from the stage.

The Yellow Card: A yellow card used by a judge in disapproval of an offensive scene. The yellow card automatically deducts one point from the team's score.

Lollies/Minties: Candies thrown to audience members during time-outs or as a thank-you for a suggestion.

Trudy Scrumptious: A six-foot-tall lollie fairy created by John Moorwood to throw minties.

The Sin Bin/Sin Bag: A large drawstring bag or garbage can in which to place offending audience members or players.

Otto: A huge, four-wheeled garbage bin that is rolled out with lid chomping in anticipation of "eating" an offensive player.

Moment of the Match: The biggest physical yield of the match, selected by the judges and replayed in slow motion.

The Second Bell: A large cowbell run by the timekeeper when only ten seconds remain in the match.

The Cranston Cup: A trophy awarded at the end of the Cranston Cup season, named after Lamont Cranston—a fictitious character [the Shadow] created by Dennis Warkins.

The Wheel: A chocolate wheel spun by team captains to randomly decide which game will be played. Note: consolation prizes are attached to the wheel (plastic toys, minties and the grand prize—a matchbox car).

The Book: An entire book of theatresports suggestions used by the compere for the team.

The Board: A small, portable board used as a basic set. The names of the games are written on it in separate sections of one-, two- and three-minute games.

VANCOUVER SUBMISSIONS

Ask For: Getting a suggestion from the audience.

Ass Clanger: A scene that's going so poorly your asshole clangs shut (also known as an "assburner").

Corpsing: Laughing at your own jokes in a poorly suppressed snicker.

Dead Audience: A quiet and unresponsive audience.

Hacking: To put down an audience member or a fellow improvisor. Sometimes effective for hecklers.

Handle: The specific game applied to a scene. (e.g. "We just did a Word At A Time. Now let's do a Status Reversal.")

Loose Cannon: A wild, out-of-control improvisor who can destroy a scene, props, or inflict bodily harm on another improvisor.

Mugging: Taking a face-making aside to the audience.

Pimping: Setting someone up to do something extraordinary and possibly outside the reality of the scene in order to get a laugh at their expense. (e.g. Two people discover a note in a bottle. "It's in your native Russian. You read it." "Okay, but you'll have to do your famous 'Note Reading Dance.")

Postmortem: The company discussion after a show.

Stealing Focus: Insisting on being the centre of attention either inside or outside of a scene (while on the bench).

Stepping Out: Breaking the reality of the scene.

Wanking: Adding nothing to a scene except being self-indulgent and cute to make the audience love you.

We killed/It killed: A brilliant scene.

SEATTLE SUBMISSIONS

Beat: A point of punctuation within a scene.

*Cancelling: Setting up a situation, then neutralizing it. (e.g. "The phone is ringing!" Picks up phone. Hangs up. "There was nobody there.")

*Gossip: A substitute for action. Talking about something that has happened, or is happening offstage. (e.g. "You should see my new plane. It's over there. [points offstage] It has gold wings . . . ")

*Hedging: Avoiding narrative development with talking or actions. (e.g. Having to tell a patient bad news, you begin with, "Have a seat. How are you feeling? I suppose you're wondering why I called you here?")

*Instant Trouble: Immediate action that establishes conflict but doesn't establish narrative. (e.g. Suddenly turning into a werewolf.)

*Never-ending Story: A story that continues to introduce new ideas to the point of being unable to tie the narrative together.

*Sidetracking: Finding activities to do to avoid doing what you established in the beginning. (e.g. You set off to fix your car, but seeing the garage is a mess, you decide to clean it. You begin to clean and find an old photo album. You look at pictures. And so on.)

Talking Heads: A scene that becomes void of action and consists of improvisors onstage talking, not doing.

NEW YORK SUBMISSIONS

Waffling: Accepting an offer but not furthering the action of a scene. Leaving all the work to your partner, making him look bad. (e.g. "Okay, I guess I'll dig the hole. Uh, how do you do it?")

Driving: When a player refuses to let another player's ideas effect a scene. When a player does everything. (e.g. "FIRE! Somebody get a fire extinguisher! I'll get it! Look, a baby on a fire escape! I'll save him!" Etc.)

Bad Mime: Poor mime technique and/or failure to recognize the established imaginary objects and environments in a scene. (e.g. Walking through a table or a wall.)

Terminology marked with an asterisk indicates topics that have been discussed by Keith Johnstone in his book Impro: Improvisation and the Theatre *(l979, London, Methuen) as well as in a series of newsletters published by the Loose Moose Theatre Company. For more information we refer readers to these publications.*

The Oral History of Theatresports

CHRONOLOGY 1977 – 1992

The following chronology has been compiled from the Loose Moose Archives and submissions from theatresports companies around the world. In our search for this timeline we found that the "mists of time" had taken their toll on both memories and printed documentation—some dates and locations being as fleeting as the memory of an amazing theatresports scene. We hope that this chronology illustrates the global spread and development of theatresports over the first fifteen or so years of its history.

1977

Calgary – The Loose Moose Theatre Company: First Impro Show at the University of Calgary.

1978

Calgary – The Loose Moose Theatre Company: First public theatresports match, Pumphouse Theatre, February. First season Rubber Chicken Playoff, April. Loose Moose is incorporated as a society on June 29.

Denmark – Turnus Players: Keith introduces theatresports while teaching at the Copenhagen State Theatre School. The month of June is established as Theatresports Month.

1979

Calgary – The Loose Moose Theatre Company: First full season of theatresports. First Innercity Tournament with Arete Mime.

1980

Calgary – The Loose Moose Theatre Company: First Annual Inner-city Invitational Tournament. Theatresports Hamlet, Pumphouse Theatre, Calgary.

Vancouver – Vancouver Theatresports League: First theatresports late-night games, City Stage, May. First Interprovincial Tournament, Calgary in Vancouver. Calgary wins 172-165.

1981

Calgary – The Loose Moose Theatre Company: First Intercity Tournament, Vancouver in Calgary, May. Loose Moose moves to the SIMPLEX, August. Theatresports is included as a Cultural Event in the Alberta Summer Games, Lethbridge.

Vancouver – Vancouver Theatresports League: First Valentine's Day Theatresports Tournament. Canadian Invitational Theatresports Tournament. Calgary wins 199-189.

Edmonton – Edmonton Theatresports: First Season of Theatresports, Theatre Network.

Toronto – Theatresports Toronto: Keith goes to Toronto for an initial workshop, December.

1982

Calgary – The Loose Moose Theatre Company: Greater Calgary Theatresports Tournament. JUDAH BEN HUR: The Epic, produced at Loose Moose. Alberta Winter Games, Lloydminster. Sports Outreach Program continues until February 1988.

Vancouver – Vancouver Theatresports League: Vancouver Theatresports Tournament. Vancouver vs. Calgary 137-132. Vancouver Theatresports Hamlet, October.

Toronto – Theatresports Toronto: Theatresports begins, Adelaide Court Theatre, February. Moves to Toronto Free Theatre (Monday nights). Moves to Habourfront (Wednesday nights). Establishes Free Workshops (every Monday).

Seattle – Seattle Theatresports: First Public Performance, Peking Restaurant.

New York – Theatresports New York (TSNY): Introductory workshop at the Ensemble Studio.

1983

Calgary – The Loose Moose Theatre Company: Theatresports Players Association. The Audience Team makes the move to Toronto.

Vancouver – Vancouver Theatresports League: First Annual Sunshine Coast Theatresports Tournament, Gibson's Landing (Vancouver, Calgary, Victoria, Seattle, Gibson's Landing).

Seattle – Seattle Theatresports: Weekly performances, Swannies Comedy Underground. First Inter-city Tournament, Vancouver in Seattle. Participants in the Bumbershoot Fall Festival of the Arts.

1984

Calgary – The Loose Moose Theatre Company. Loose Moose goes to the International Festival of Fools. New York and the Quinzaine Festival in Quebec City. First National Tournament, The Greater Calgary Theatresports Open (Vancouver, Edmonton and Toronto in Calgary). 'Myth Toronto' wins.

Vancouver – Vancouver Theatresports League: Second Annual Sunshine Coast Theatresports Tournament, Gibson's Landing (Vancouver, Calgary, Victoria, Seattle, Gibson's Landing).

Edmonton – Edmonton Theatresports: Inner-City Golden Nose Theatresports Tournament.

Toronto – Theatresports Toronto: Survival of the Wittiest—First Theatresports National Tournament.

Seattle – Seattle Theatresports: Incorporated as Seattle Theatresports. Offering workshops in Seattle High Schools.

New York – Theatresports New York (TSNY): First regular season of theatresports, Terry Schreiber Studio.

1985

Edmonton – Edmonton Theatresports: Alberta Winter Games Theatresports Event, Gold and Silver Medals. Golden Nose Tournament. Theatresports Classic Movie Nights

Toronto – Theatresports Toronto: Toronto International Children's Festival participants.

Seattle – Seattle Theatresports: New City Director's Festival.

New York – Theatresports New York (TSNY): First Tournament, The Stanislavski Open.

Australia: First theatresports game played at the Belvoir Street Theatre in Sydney. First National Tournament played for the Cranston Cup in Sydney.

Hobart Tasmania: Performing Arts Club, Backspace Theatre.

Perth: Deckchair Theatre forms and theatresports begins.

1986

Vancouver – Vancouver Theatresports League: Organises EXPO '86 Tournaments in Vancouver. May 17–19, Canadian Tournament. Calgary, Edmonton, Toronto, Vancouver. June 30, July 1–2, Can/Am Tournament. Seattle, New York, Vancouver. August 1–4—International. Australia, England, Sweden, Vancouver, Calgary, New York, Seattle.

Edmonton – Edmonton Theatresports: Alberta Winter Games Theatresports Events, Gold and Silver Medals. Golden Nose Theatresports Tournament.

Toronto – Theatresports Toronto: First Theatresports Toronto Comedy Summit.

Seattle – Seattle Theatresports: First Ever Improvathon (24 Hours).

New York – Theatresports New York (TSNY): Established the Outreach Program—performances to charitable organizations.

San Francisco – Bay Area Theatresports (BATS): Group's Formation. First Public Theatresports Game, Zephyr Theatre.

Norway – Oslo: First public theatresports games are played in Oslo.

Australia: Theatresports Series filmed in Sydney on ABC–TV for broadcast in March 1987.

1987

Calgary – The Loose Moose Theatre Company: First Theatresports Newsletter.

Edmonton – Edmonton Theatresports: Golden Nose Tournament.

Toronto – Theatresports Toronto: Theatresports National Tournament.

Seattle – Seattle Theatresports: Move to Group Theatre. 2nd Improvathon (24 Hours). Changed name to Unexpected Productions.

New York – Theatresports New York (TSNY): Established as a nonprofit organisation. Hosted TSNY Improv Festival (Seattle, Calgary, Edmonton, Toronto).

San Francisco – Bay Area Theatresports (BATS): Regular Monday Night Performances, New Performance Gallery. First Inner-City Tournament. Inter-city Player Exchanges with LA and Seattle.

Rotterdam – Theatresport "Lawine": Group formation and beginning of studio training sessions.

London: Informal theatresports at the Edinburgh Festival Theatresports begins at the Donmore Warehouse, London.

Australia: Next Wave Festival held in Melbourne launches theatresports in the schools

New Zealand: First match held at the Court Theatre in Christchurch, South Island. First North Island match in Auckland at the Pumphouse in Takapuna, videotaped by Television New Zealand. Theatresports television coverage airs on TV One on "Kaleidoscope."

1988

Calgary – The Loose Moose Theatre Company: Olympic Tournament, Calgary, February (Calgary, Edmonton, Vancouver, Toronto, New York, Seattle, England, Denmark, Sweden, Australia). Loose Moose All-Star Impro Show begins.

Edmonton – Edmonton Theatresports: Pupil's Choice High School Tournament. International Invitational Golden Nose Theatresports Tournament. Rapid Fire Theatre forms.

Toronto – Theatresports Toronto: The Comedy Summit: Theatresports Toronto International Comedy Improv Festival.

San Francisco – Bay Area Theatresports (BATS): Participates in the San Francisco International Vaudeville Festival. Acquired office and studio space.

New York – Theatresports New York (TSNY): Move to the Westside Arts Theatre.

Denmark – Turnus Players: Established the Impro Café.

Rotterdam – Theatresport "Lawine": First performance in the studio for an invited audience. Keith teaches a workshop for drama teachers in Holland.

London – Theatresports UK: Keith helps settle dispute between theatresports groups, and Theatresports UK is born.

Australia: Theatresports played in every state. EXPO Tournament, Brisbane in July (Calgary, Vancouver, Edmonton, New York, Denmark, New Zealand, Australia).

New Zealand – United Theatresports: The United Building Society provides a three-year sponsorship for theatresports. National Games as held at the James Hay Theatre in Christchurch. One-hour TV special on the National Games is aired on TVNZ.

1989

Calgary – The Loose Moose Theatre Company: "How It Was" premières under the direction of Keith for a six-month run funded by Canada Council Explorations Program. First Loose Moose International Improvisational School (Students from Toronto, Vancouver, Holland, New Zealand, Australia, Italy, New York).

Edmonton – Edmonton Theatresports: First International Tournament.

Toronto – Theatresports Toronto: The Coors Light International Theatresports Tournament (San Francisco, London, Calgary, Toronto, Seattle). First Shakespeare in the Pond *(King Lear).*

Seattle – Seattle Theatresports: Move to the Intiman Playhouse.

San Francisco – Bay Area Theatresports (BATS): Begin "Late Night" Series, Long Form Improvisation Formats.

New York – Theatresports New York (TSNY): 2nd Stanislavski Open, twenty teams over five weeks. Begin Junior Varsity League for Inner-city kids. Performing in schools under Young Audiences NY. Begin *Freestyle Monday, Play by Play, The Natural Coffeehouse Radio Hour, Real Life: The Improv.*

Rotterdam – Theatresport "Lawine": Keith returns for a second workshop, and more theatresports organizations form (Amsterdam, Utrecht). First public performance against Amsterdam at the Spinoza Café in Amsterdam. Inter-City play continues within the first four groups for the first season of play.

Germany – Theatresport LTT – Tubingen (Landestheater Wurtemberg-Hohenzollern): Theatresports arrives in Germany via Denmark.

Norway – Oslo: Oslo plays in the Nordic Theatresports Championships held in Copenhagen. Regular theatresports matches held at the Central Theatre in Oslo.

Australia: Theatresports School Program continues in Sydney under the direction of the Belvoir Street Theatre.

New Zealand – United Theatresports: United Theatresports begins their School Programme in forty-nine secondary schools throughout the country. United Theatresports National Final is held in Auckland at the Mercury Theatre. First United Theatresports Secondary Schools Festival is held in Wellington.

1990

Toronto – Theatresports Toronto: Theatresports Toronto 3rd International Comedy Summit.

Seattle – Seattle Theatresports: Cream of Wit Theatresports Tournament.

New York – Theatresports New York (TSNY): The American Improv Festival 1990.

Rotterdam – Theatresport "Lawine": First Dutch Open Theatresports Championship (eight teams, including Brussels and London). The Defeat of Giant Big Nose, written by Keith Johnstone, directed by Tony Totino, performed at the Teatro Fantasico Festival, Rotterdam.

London – Theatresports UK: First tournament in the UK. Theatresports UK formulates constitution

Germany – Theatresport LTT – Tubingen (Landestheater Wurtemberg-Hohenzollern): First public performance of theatresports.

Norway – Oslo: Olso plays in the Nordic Theatresports Championship held in Stockholm. Four members attend the International Improvisation School in Calgary. Theatresports moves to Slurpen (The Slurp), a former soup kitchen converted into a theatre in the eastern part of Oslo. Beginner classes are open to the public for the first time.

New Zealand – United Theatresports: Auckland hosts the

1990 International Challenge as part of the Commonwealth Games (Australia, Canada, New Zealand and U.S. participants). During a United Theatresports demonstration at the Commonwealth Games, Prince Edward participates in a Moving Bodies scene. 1990 International Challenge Tour plays in North and South Island cities and finishes with performances at the New Zealand International Festival of the Arts in Wellington. 2nd United Theatresports Secondary Schools Festival is held in Christchurch with ten centres represented. The United Theatresports National Final. A one-hour TV special is aired on *10 AM,* featuring the highlights of the National Final.

1991

Edmonton – Edmonton Theatresports: International Tournament at the Fringe Festival (Edmonton, Calgary, Los Angeles, Orlando, Portland, Rotterdam, Chattanooga, Auckland, San Francisco).

Toronto – Theatresports Toronto: 4th International Comedy Summit (Toronto, Halifax, New York, London, Tubingen).

Seattle – Seattle Theatresports: Opened own theatre, Market Theatre.

San Francisco – Bay Area Theatresports (BATS): First International Tournament in Bay Area.

New York – Theatresports New York (TSNY): Moved to Studio A at the John Houseman Theatre. Stanislavski Open. International Theatresports Festival 1991, Pace Downtown Theatre (Los Angeles, San Francisco, Seattle, New York, Toronto, Calgary, Australia, New Zealand, Vancouver).

Rotterdam – Theatresport "Lawine": Theatresports groups playing in Rotterdam, Amsterdam, Nijmegen, Zwolle, Utrecht, Alkmaar. First International Theatresports Match. Lawine vs. BIL (Belgische Improvisatie Liga) from Brussels, Belgium.

Germany – Theatresport LTT – Tubingen (Landestheater Wurtemberg-Hohenzollern): First interstate competition, Tubingen vs. Dresden.

Norway – Oslo: Oslo hosts the Nordic Theatresports Championships, and a Finnish team competes for the first time. Three members compete in the New York International Theatresports Festival.

Australia: Theatresports Inc. is established in Sydney by the players with separate Board of Directors and is still played at the Belvoir Street Theatre.

1992

Norway – Oslo: Tony Totino becomes artistic director of Theatresports in Oslo. Experimentation begins with new formats such as The Life Game and The Impro Show. Members perform at conferences, clubs and schools as well as teaching classes around the country.

And the development and growth of theatresports goes on.

A communiqué from those attending a theatresports tournament in L.A. has informed us that South Africa is now competing at the international level and Zimbabwe has been introduced to the game. In addition, the National Association of Theatresports (USA) has designated as objectives a desire to hold a "Female Improvisors Symposia" in Seattle, and to place theatresports new on the computer network (e-mail and Internet).

In all our wanderings, we never managed to be in the same place at the same time as any of the Danish theatresports players, so we decided to include this letter sent to the Dutch chapter of improvisors from Turnus Theatre in Denmark .

Letter from Denmark

Dear brothers and sisters in improvisation (though sons and daughters would probably be more appropriate).

Greetings from the oldest surviving theatresports players in Europe. We have been thrilled by your first newsletters—it's wonderful that you at the Lawine are setting up a European network of theatresports groups. Our theatre—the Turnus Theatre—is a Copenhagen based fringe theatre, which has existed since 1970. We are a professional group staging, on an average, two adult and one children's productions every year. From the very beginning we have preferred—rather than to stage a finished playscript—to produce our own shows through improvisation. So in the late seventies when Keith Johnstone came regularly to teach at the Copenhagen State Theatre School, he managed to give us some workshops in improvisation and mask work (we subsequently produced a highly successful version of his Robinson Crusoe). In 1978 he was more than usually animated because he had just started something back in Calgary which he called theatresports and which he thought we should try as well . . . since then we alternately adored him like a god and wished to see him burn in hell.

Unlike most other groups working with theatresports we have always staged it for one month every year (June is the theatresports season in Copenhagen!), simply because as a professional theatre we have too many other obligations throughout the year. Over the last couple of years, however, we have developed a very successful Impro Café—a late-night smaller show with four or five players, a pianist and a compere. In Impro Café as in the first half of our theatresports shows we play suggestions from the audience exclusively (the audience write their suggestions on slips of paper which are subsequently collected in a hat). The first half is judged by the audience (the so-called Danish game), not as Keith claims by having them shout for their team, but by having them hold up red or blue cards (as we play in a boxing ring we have, of course, a red and blue corner for the two teams). In the second half, the two teams take turns at challenging each other and at the very end of the show we have a very popular "betting session." In the interval between the first and the second half, the audience go to a betting booth and fill in slips indicating which team they think will win five separate games. These five betting games vary from year to year—this year, for example, we played Arms, Hat Game, Emotions, Musical Suggestions and Reverse.

The second half and, of course, the betting session are judged by professional judges (one can imagine the chaos if the audience were to judge the games they have placed their bets on). Keith has always taken pleasure in chiding us about a national game between Denmark and Sweden in which we let the audience judge the first half.

To us this mirrors a central schizophrenia in theatresports: Should it be primarily sports or theatre? Should we try to set up as many rules as possible in order to ensure that "the best team wins"—or should we say, "Fuck the result! Give the audience as good a show as possible"? In our ripe age we tend to hold with the latter view (though it still hurts to lose, of course!) and we have the feeling that this is shared by other Scandinavian theatresports centres. When we played in Stockhold against Sweden a couple of years ago, we were clearly allowed to win by the judges and when we staged the Nordic Championships last year in Copenhagen we made it more or less clear to the judges that we did not want to win our own homemade trophy! (it was atrocious!)—perhaps it all boils down to two basic considerations:

1) A good impro show requires players that enjoy themselves.

2) The fewer rules and the less competition, the more enjoyment for the players.

That's all from us now. Let us hear from you if you are ever in Copenhagen and keep up the good work at "Eureka!"

–On behalf of the Turnus players: Gunner Froberg

Epilogue . . . 1995

The Sound of a microphone being blown into

Kathleen: Test, test . . . we got it. Okay, this is Kathleen Foreman and Clem Martini, and this is the epilogue to *Something Like A Drug.*

Clem: So how do you feel?

Kathleen: That's exactly what I was going to ask. . . .

Clem: Ah, ah, I asked first though. I asked first, so I get the first answer. So how do *you* feel having come to the finish of this book?

Kathleen: I feel very excited about this collection of stories coming together in a final form. I mean, I have been excited about this project from the very beginning. I've loved talking to all the people. That's been just incredible. And seeing the patterns emerge, the similarities between people's experiences. People from opposite sides of the world have come to theatresports in a variety of different ways and, yet, have shared experiences under this huge umbrella of a beast we call theatresports, and that's been fascinating for me.

And I'm relieved that it's coming to an end. Finally.

Clem: Because it could go on forever.

Kathleen: It could go on forever because we could go on talking to new players.

Clem: I think that's really interesting, that it *could* go on forever because the game, even as we speak, is being taken up in Germany, it's moving into Eastern Europe. Every time I get up to Loose Moose there's mention of yet another place it's going. Now it's in Korea, now it's in South Africa, now it's in Finland, and so it's one of the few things . . . and it's fascinating to see this happening during a recession when everything else is contracting . . . one of the few things in the Arts that is *expanding*. And that may be significant , who knows, that may be significant because other theatres, certainly professional theatres *are* contracting. In Canada the question asked today seems to be "Can theatres continue to exist as they have in the past?" And this *isn't* the question being asked of theatresports.

I can't think of anything like it, really. I mean, it's interesting looking at this, how quickly it's moving, how this form has moved like a . . . like a . . . I know I said virus in my introduction to the book, and it *is* like a virus. It's not like someone said "I'm going to take it around the world, I'm going to make sure it goes from here to here to here." It's always word of mouth. It's always someone says "I like this. I saw this." and they take it with them. And the moment it plants its foot on soil it kind of takes off. That's what happened in Australia, that's what's happening in Europe.

Kathleen: It's *people* connected.

Clem: And it's also fascinating looking at this because it's about *passion*. It's kind of been a big soap opera. Everyone so passionately connected to this thing. There's not enough money in doing it right now, that people do it for the money, they all do it because they're *hooked*, right?

Kathleen: Yeah, they love it. "I'm hooked." "I'm addicted." That's the way they always put it.

Clem: It's a way of truly expressing *themselves*, and so everywhere they're passionate about their ownership.

Kathleen: It's also intriguing that theatresports reflects where it is. It becomes a . . . a mirror of the culture, or the microculture, that it settles in. I mean, the incredible expansiveness of sexuality in the roles that the players take on in San Francisco is not like anywhere else, and in Western Canada we are accused of being red necked and sexist, very often, in the theatresports community but . . . that's *where* we are. Yet whenever these people, no matter what their particular style is, come together they're still able to play.

Clem: It's become another language. Someone said that they can go from country to country and continent to continent and say "I'm an Improvisor" and they're welcomed. It's like a big family, or a brotherhood, or . . . or a language. You know, like I say "I can speak Improviseze" . . .

Kathleen: "I know how to not block. I can tell a story. I can advance a narrative."

Clem: That is so . . . weird. I can't think of anything else that exists like that today. Where else is there an art form where you immediately are welcomed that way? You can't say to someone "Hi, I'm a painter. Take me in." But among improvisors *that happens.*

Kathleen: And you can play. Maybe it's more like a sport in that.

Clem: Or a religion.

Kathleen: Maybe.

Clem: And it all started . . . here. Given the subject of this book, maybe we should conclude with a bit of A Word At A Time.

Kathleen: One

Clem: day

Kathleen: we

Clem: started

Kathleen: talking.

Clem: We

Kathleen: discovered

Clem: that

Kathleen: we

Clem: found

Kathleen: mystery

Clem: in

Kathleen: our

Clem: lives

Kathleen: because

Clem: the

Kathleen: experience

Clem: of

Kathleen: theatresports

Clem: was

Kathleen: intriguing

Clem: so

Kathleen: we

Clem: continued

Kathleen: asking

Clem: questions

Kathleen: of

Clem: other

Kathleen: people.

Clem: They

Kathleen: told

Clem: us

Kathleen: things

Clem: about

Kathleen: themselves

Clem: and

Kathleen: their

Clem: love

Kathleen: of

Clem: theatresports

Kathleen: and

Clem: improvisation

Kathleen: so

Clem: we

Kathleen: finally

Clem: put

Kathleen: it

Clem: all

Kathleen: in

Clem: this

Kathleen: book

Clem: and

Kathleen: here

Clem: it

Kathleen: is.

Clem: The

Kathleen: end.